Marking the End:

Sense and Absence
in the Gospel of Mark

Marking the End:

Sense and Absence
in the Gospel of Mark

J. Lee Magness

Wipf and Stock Publishers
150 West Broadway • Eugene OR 97401

Marking the End:

Sense and Absence
in the Gospel of Mark

Wipf and Stock Publishers
150 West Broadway
Eugene, Oregon 97401

Marking the End: Sense and Absence in the Gospel of Mark
By Magness, J. Lee
©1986 Magness, J. Lee
ISBN: 1-57910-876-8
Publication date: January, 2002
Previously published by Scholars Press, 1986.

Previously published as Sense and Absence: Structure and
Suspension in the Ending of Mark's Gospel

CONTENTS

Chapter I

"THE REST IS SILENCE":
THE PROBLEM OF THE ENDING OF MARK

> Do you realize that that wild, atonal-sounding passage
> contains every one of the twelve chromatic tones except
> the tonic note G? What an inspired idea—all the notes
> except the tonic! It would easily pass for twentieth cen-
> tury music, if we didn't already know it was Mozart.
>
> —LEONARD BERNSTEIN[1]

In 1881 the first edition of the Greek New Testament edited by
Westcott and Hort boldly brought the text of the Gospel of Mark to
an end at 16:8 with a colon and six asterisks. This book is about those
asterisks.

The decision of the editors was both the culmination of centuries of discussion and the catalyst for further debate which continues over a century later. The implications of their decision are
obvious. Westcott and Hort were among the growing number of
scholars who had recognized that the best Greek texts of Mark
ended at 16:8 and that 16:9–20 were not originally part of the
Gospel. On the other hand the editors were confident that "for they
were afraid" did not constitute an appropriate ending even to a
sentence much less a book (hence the colon) and that more information was originally included or was intended to be included in the
book (hence the asterisks).

However obvious the implications may be, the explanation is far
from clear. In fact, that such a pivotal work as Mark should end so
suddenly, so unexpectedly, has been called "the greatest of all
literary mysteries" (Nineham: 439; Branscomb: 311). But the ending
of Mark has a way of evoking this kind of hyperbole. Whether the
analysis defends 16:9-20 as the original conclusion or assumes that

---

[1] Bernstein (1976:47) is commenting on the conclusion of the fifth movement of
Mozart's *G Minor Symphony*.

the original ending has been lost or insists that the Gospel originally ended at 16:8, the ending of Mark evokes hyperbole. Those who assume that the original ending of the Gospel is missing see the loss as "the greatest disaster in the history of the New Testament" (Branscomb: 311). "Unparalleled," "incredible," "astonishing," "nonsense"—writers exhaust the rhetoric of incredulity in their rejection of 16:1-8 as a possible conclusion (Knox: 22; Hunter: 4; Zahn: 485). Even those who insist that 16:1-8 is the original ending speak of its "weak and ineffectual character" (Weeden, 1971:102) and view it as a theological "scandal" (Kermode, 1979:67).

If the discussion of the ending of Mark has been loud, it has also been long. Eusebius (c. 260-c. 339) reported that accurate manuscripts of our second gospel ended with what we call 16:8.[2] Books and articles written in the last quarter of the twentieth century still grapple with various aspects of the problem.[3] Over a millenium and a half, through changing theological perspectives and hermeneutical approaches, from the pens of ancient Alexandrian allegorists and modern French structuralists, discussion of the shortened ending of the shortest gospel persists.

The Depth of the Problem

At issue is Mark's handling of the event around which the Christian faith revolves, the resurrection of Jesus. No canonical gospel writer actually narrates the event itself.[4] Instead Christian tradition preserves stories of appearances of Jesus to his followers, appearances whose narration replaced the unnarratable resurrection in the gospels and played a key apologetic role in early Christian theological documents. If Mark ends at 16:8 there is not only no direct description of the resurrection event; there are no post-resurrection appearances to confirm the reality of the resurrection event. The closest Mark comes to a description or an account of the resurrection or of a post-resurrection appearance is the proclamation and promise entailed in the young man's words in 16:7. As important as this statement is, it must be identified as an announcement in discourse form and distinguished from an account in narrative form.

---

[2] Eusebius records this example of early Christian textual criticism in Quaest. ad Marinum I.

[3] See, for example, titles by Kelber (1979), Petersen (1977), and Boomershine (1981b).

[4] The Gospel of Peter attempts a detailed description of the resurrection; however it might have affected its original audience, it now appears contrived and trivial.

Thus, "it is not a question of a single work or a single passage of the context, but of an entire section so essential and important, the omission of which," for most commentators, "deprives the whole Gospel of completeness" (Meyer: 197).

The fact that early testimony about Jesus focused on the crucifixion and resurrection and that the discussion of the resurrection focused on the post-resurrection appearance narratives makes their omission from Mark all the more remarkable. First, the *kerygma*, the generative core of early Christian preaching, was comprised of the death and burial and resurrection of Jesus:

> how God anointed Jesus of Nazareth with the Holy Spirit and with power; how he went about doing good and healing all that were oppressed by the devil, for God was with him. And we are witnesses to all that he did both in the country of the Jews and in Jerusalem. They put him to death by hanging him on a tree; but God raised him on the third day and made him manifest; not to all the people but to us who were chosen by God as witnesses, who ate and drank with him after he rose from the dead. And he commanded us to preach to the people, and to testify that he is the one ordained by God to be judge of the living and the dead (Acts 10:38–42).[5]

The resurrection was the climactic point of most Christian missionary communication to listeners of Jewish and Hellenistic backgrounds and what happened "after he rose" was also of crucial importance. Second, the *paradosis*, the body of Christian tradition handed down from one community to another and one generation to the next, included the resurrection and the confirming appearances:

> For I delivered to you as of first importance what I also received, that Christ died for our sins in accordance with the scriptures, that he was buried, that he was raised on the third day in accordance with the scriptures, and that he appeared to Cephas, then to the twelve. Then he appeared to more than five hundred brethren at one time, most of whom are still alive, though some have fallen asleep. Then he appeared to James, then to all the apostles. Last of all, as to one untimely born, he appeared also to me (I Corinthians 15:3–8).

---

[5] All quotations of the Bible will be taken from the *Revised Standard Version* (New York: Oxford University Press, 1946, 1952) unless otherwise stated.

Third, the Apostolic Fathers, second century advocates of the Christian faith, made much of the post-resurrection appearances as proof of the bodily resurrection.[6] The existence of Christianity, of a Christian gospel, of a Christian church, of Christian theologians and their writings, presupposes the very fact and supporting evidence which Mark omits. And even if it did not, the repeated and central use of these stories would seem to make their inclusion in Mark a foregone conclusion.

The programmatic differences between Mark and the Apostolic Fathers account for why they might use the resurrection accounts differently. Mark was not battling the docetist teachings which denied the incarnation and therefore the bodily resurrection. Neither was he tackling the important distinction between the doctrine of the immortality of the soul and that of the resurrection of the body. Still, the definitive place of the resurrection and appearance accounts in the kerygma and the paradosis as we know them makes Mark's omission striking, especially if we accept the tradition that Mark's Gospel is the (at least) indirect heir of Peter's preaching and teaching.

The Dimensions of the Problem

The problem of the ending of Mark is significant not only because it touches the nerve center of the Christian faith. It gains in significance through the wide range of issues involved. At stake are textual, grammatical, literary, and theological questions of considerable import. The arguments cluster around several options. First, is Mark 16:9–20 an inherent part of the original text of Mark or not? Was the shorter ending the original conclusion? At issue are text-critical questions, linguistic analyses, and matters of comparative theological content. Second, if vv. 9–20 are not the original ending, has the ancient conclusion been lost or did the author intend to close his Gospel at 16:8 all along? Syntactical, literary, and theological features of the text must be weighed in an attempt to choose between these options. And third, if Mark indeed originally ended at 16:8, what was the impact and the import of such a conclusion on the first and succeeding readers? A whole array of literary and theological perspectives have been brought to bear on this question.

---

[6] For two among many examples of this emphasis see Ignatius, "The Epistle of Ignatius to the Smyrneans," and Justin, "Fragments of the Lost Work of Justin on the Resurrection," in *The Ante-Nicene Fathers*, Vol. 1.

The dimensions of this debate must be explored in some detail as a background to the present study.

The first matter of debate is the integrity of the traditional ending of Mark. The longer ending, Mark 16:9–20, is found in many ancient manuscripts and many modern translations.[7] An old Latin manuscript, Bobiensis (k), adds a shorter ending to verse 8: "But they reported briefly to Peter and to those with him, all that they had been told. And after this, Jesus himself sent out by means of them, from east to west, the sacred and imperishable proclamation of eternal salvation." Some modern scholars have defended the longer ending in whole or in part, and some accept the shorter ending.[8] But 16:9–20 is rejected as the original ending of Mark's Gospel by most of its students.

Many factors militate against the acceptance of the traditional ending:

1. Manuscript evidence. Codices Sinaiticus and Vaticanus, representatives of old and reliable manuscript traditions, lack these verses, as does the Western text Bobiensis. As mentioned above, Eusebius claimed that "accurate" manuscripts of Mark stopped at 16:8.

2. Transcription. "It is inconceivable that any copyist would have omitted the twelve final verses of the Gospel of Mark if they were original" (Bratcher and Nida: 519).

3. Attestation. Origen, Tertullian, Cyprian, and Cyril of Jerusalem are some of the early Christian writers who show no acquaintance with the longer ending.

4. Vocabulary. Statistical analysis of words employed in 16:9–20 has demonstrated that the verses were written by another author. The results of this research have been disputed, but most Marcan scholars have become convinced that the vocabulary is too different for the conclusion to have been written by the same author.[9]

5. Style. Most critics agree that the style of the longer ending is alien to the body of the Gospel; verses 9–20 are "concise and barren," lacking the "vivid and lifelike details" characteristic of Mark (Bratcher and Nida: 519–521).

---

[7] For details of the textual readings see Aland, et al., *The Greek New Testament* (United Bible Societies, 1975), and Metzger, 1971:122–128.

[8] Farmer presents the case for the integrity of 16:9–20. Linnemann is more selective within 9–20. Aland opts for the short ending.

[9] Morganthaler's work established the lexical dissmilarity, although Farmer and Linnemann have disputed his statistics.

6. Content. The last twelve verses have a patchwork nature, seemingly sewn together from the remnants of Luke-Acts and perhaps Matthew and John, and contain details which are inconsistent with Mark's themes and his depiction of Jesus. On both theological and narrative grounds, these verses are uncharacteristic of the body of Mark's Gospel.

So although 16:9–20 may be very old and may have been added to Mark relatively soon after the composition of the Gospel, the preponderance of modern opinion suggests that it is not the original ending. Even if it could be proved that 16:9–20 was the original ending of Mark, this present study would still, of course, be necessary. There would remain the matter of those readers whose copies of Mark did end at verse 8. What would they have made of this story of Jesus, ending in fear and flight from an empty tomb and an earnest young man? But overwhelming evidence demands that we reject verses 9–20 and look elsewhere for the original ending.

The second matter of debate involves the options left after 16:9–20 has been discounted as the original conclusion of Mark. Either the original ending has been somehow separated from the Gospel and lost to memory or the author intended to close his narration with the words in 16:8. Several obstacles stand in the way of accepting 16:8 as a coherent conclusion. One is a grammatical controversy at the heart of which is the tiny Greek conjunction *gar*. Can a Greek sentence, much less a paragraph or a whole book, end with a conjunction? A post-positive conjunction is never the first word in a clause, but can it ever be the last, as it would be if Mark ends with "for they were afraid" *(ephobounto gar)*. Most commentators thought it improbable if not impossible; for one thing, no examples existed. Older grammarians also questioned the use of "they were afraid" without some objective complement. Moffatt signalled his agreement with the prevailing opinion by translating the last words of Mark, "for they were afraid of--." But recently uncovered examples from Greek literature have demonstrated that although such a construction may be "barbarous" (Perrin, 1977:16–17), it is clearly possible for a Greek sentence to end with a conjunction like *gar*.[10]

A second obstacle to the acceptance of 16:8 as the intended ending involves a broader literary question. Even if a book could

---

[10] Lightfoot (1938:11–16; 1950:80–97, 106–116) defends the use of a final *gar* by appealing to literary parallels in classical Greek, the Septuagint, early Christian writers, and Mark itself. Danker and van der Horst have produced separate studies supporting his contention. More recently Boomershine confirmed the usage.

end with a conjunction, is such an inconclusive ending as 16:1–8 offers the reader a logical or likely way to conclude a coherent and complete narrative? One might ask at this point if a literary analysis, including the search for and identification of sophisticated literary devices, is appropriate to the study of Mark. A sympathetic literary critic has put the problem nicely:

> A main obstacle to our accepting "for they were scared" as the true ending, and going about our business of finding internal validation for it, is simply that Mark is, or was, not supposed to be capable of the kinds of refinement we should have to postulate (Kermode, 1979:68).

There are at least two responses we can make to this legitimate hesitation. First, literary devices are literary devices, regardless if they are used consciously or unconsciously, regardless if they have been recognized and catalogued by contemporary literary critics.[11] Second, the Gospel of Mark, for all its simplicity, is also characterized by amazing literary sophistication (Rhoads and Michie: 1). Claiming the right and necessity of advancing on literary-critical grounds, we return to the question of the literary appropriateness of Mark's ending.

As early as 1909, commentators argued that for Mark to have intentionally concluded at 16:8 would have been "in singular contradiction to literary history of all ages" (Zahn: 485). W. L. Knox (1942:22–23) pursued this comparative line of reasoning.

> To suppose that Mark originally intended to end his Gospel this way implies both that he was totally indifferent to the canons of popular story-telling, and that by pure accident he happened to hit on a conclusion which suits the technique of a highly sophisticated type of modern literature. The odds against such a coincidence (even if we could for a moment entertain the idea that Mark was indifferent to canons which he observes scrupulously elsewhere in his Gospel) seem to me to be so enormous as not to be worth considering.

Knox elaborated on his claim by delineating the conventional endings of ancient biographies and quasi-biographical books. The genre "demands that you must round off your incident properly, leaving

---

[11] See Freedman's (1977:12) defense of identifying "modern" literary devices in ancient literature.

nothing to the imagination" (1942–15). More specifically, Knox argued that since Mark rounds off all his shorter narratives it is inconceivable that he would not round off the larger story.

Many writers have answered Knox either directly or indirectly and from a variety of viewpoints. Some question the basic genre identification of gospel with biography.[12] Boomershine (1981lb:214) answers Knox's rejection of 16:8 on internal grounds by showing that the final sentence fits a pattern in Mark which includes 1) concluding narrative comments to explain a puzzling element, 2) concluding inside views which illuminate a character's emotions, and 3) concluding short sentences which draw the event to a close. Redaction criticism points up a blind spot created by Knox's exclusively form-critical perspective and thereby a weakness in Knox's external argument from literary comparison:[13] "To argue that Mark must have followed the same procedure as other Christian writers who wrote similar compositions violates the integrity of Mark by forcing it to harmonize with its literary descendants" (Weeden, 1971:46). What is true of Mark's relation to his literary descendants is also true if to a lesser extent of the Gospel writer's relation to his literary forebears.

Generic comparisons aside, other literary objections have been raised. Lacking post-resurrection appearances of Jesus to his frightened followers, 16:1–8 strikes some as simply too sad an ending for a book which purports to be about the "good news" of Jesus Christ (Mark 1:1). Others claim that these allusive even enigmatic verses present too great a challenge to the literary sophistication of Mark's readers. Simply from the point of view of good story-telling, still others object to the many loose ends left dangling at verse 8. Each of these objections has an answer. The mere fact of the resurrection—which is asserted in Mark—is sufficient to characterize the Gospel as "good news." The ability of the reader to fill in a few facts which have been carefully and consistently foreshadowed is hardly the mark of great literary sophistication and is an every-day reading skill which has not been sufficiently taken into account by interpreters of Mark. As to the matter of "loose ends," the announcement of the young man/angel in 16:7 ties several neat narrative knots in the

[12] On the other hand, Charles Talbert's recent book, *What is a Gospel?* (Fortress, 1977), defends the connection between gospel and ancient biography.

[13] Knox (1942:23) actually says: "In any case the supposition credits him with a degree of originality which would invalidate the whole method of form criticism."

threads woven throughout the text. Each of the objections has an answer; but questions persist.

Before leaving these literary issues, two summary assertions must be made as background to the study which follows. First, Knox's thesis is unsatisfactory. He compares Mark only to ancient biography, which may not be the best and is certainly not the only type of literature with which the readers of Mark would have been familiar. He implies that full narrative closure is characteristic of all ancient biography; this implication may not be completely true and is certainly not true of other types of ancient literature. Second, the widespread opinion that ancient writers and readers were not sophisticated enough to produce or understand "open endings" is subject to question. A survey of ancient Hebrew, Greek, and Roman literature reveals just the opposite. The chapters which follow explore these matters through a fresh analysis of ancient literary conclusions.

A theological issue is the third point of contention in the discussion over whether 16:1–8 or some now lost addition was the original ending of Mark. To many commentators a conclusion at 16:8 is theologically unthinkable. Weeden (1971:102–103) assumes that two first-century theologians whom we call Matthew and Luke "found the grave story to be insufficient and even problematic as proclamation and convincing verification of the Easter event." Modern theologians have been similarly dissatisfied. The most obvious omission is a post-resurrection appearance story, the means used by other gospel writers and early Christian theologians to verify the unnarratable resurrection event and to close off their narrative of Jesus' life. But not all of the gospels narrate the ascension of Jesus, for instance; and that event quickly found an important place in kerygmatic and creedal formulations in the early church. One of the questions which must be asked and which this study addresses is not, "What might Mark have meant by how he might have ended?," but "What sense can we make of how Mark did end?" Other theological oddities are the notes of fear and flight and silence on which the Gospel ends. With no subsequent narrative of faith and following and proclamation to balance them, the short ending amounts to a "theological scandal" (Kermode, 1979:67) which many commentators find inexplicable and untenable. But fear and silence are characteristic responses to the miraculous in Mark. A thorough survey of these interrelated functions in Marcan miracle stories demonstrates that fear and silence are not theologically impossible as some have suggested.

Those who find the literary or theological difficulties insurmountable and are forced to reject 16:8 as a coherent conclusion are not without solutions to the problem.[14] A number of theories have been advanced which steer a course between the "scandal" of an ending at 16:8 and the textual problems of the longer ending (16:9–20). Most scholars are content to speculate about what happened to the lost ending. Mark may have been prevented from finishing the document: his death, a change in circumstances, or some other interruption may have intervened. Mark may not have wished to complete the work, intending a sequel. The last portion of the manuscript may have been lost through accidental damage or mutilation. Some even theorize a deliberate suppression and excision of the original ending to avoid what some early Christian teachers might have perceived to be a contradiction with Matthew, the "normative" gospel.[15]

Attempts have been made to reconstruct the "missing" ending. Some posit the lost account of a post-resurrection appearance in Galilee to satisfy the instruction of the young man in 16:7. Others suggest that the omitted fragment would have focused on the activities of the women and an apostolic visit to the empty tomb. It has been argued that the lost ending would have looked like Matthew 28:9–10, which may be Mark's original ending in a slightly altered or expanded form. Moule (1955:58–59) makes bold to suggest the actual wording of the long-lost ending: "and immediately they told the disciples about these things."

These theories and the assumption behind them—that for literary and theological reasons Mark could and would not have ended his Gospel at 16:8—do not invalidate the purpose and necessity of the present study for several reasons. First, these reconstructions are at best indications of how a modern Biblical scholar might have ended Mark; no "lost" ending exists and remains hypothetical. While reconstruction is an interesting exercise the more important task is to forge an interpretation suitable to the ending of the book, not construct an ending to the book which suits our interpretation.

---

[14] The list of those who reject an intended closure at verse 8 includes Knox, Trompf, Taylor, Hort, Swete, Moffatt, Burkitt, Streeter, Branscomb, Schniewind, Zahn, Rawlinson, Bultmann, Cranfield, Hunter, Cadoux, Jeremias, Moule, and Farrer.

[15] Farmer (1974:62f) examines this proposition; it is advocated by Jeremias and refuted by Branscomb.

Second, the reconstructions provide the evidence for what succeeding chapters will demonstrate and argue—that without actually narrating a conclusion, the author supplies enough information for the careful reader to sense the absent ending. Third, even if we should accept the theory of damage or loss or mutilation or suppression, we must again affirm that, at least for those who read Sinaiticus or Vaticanus, Mark did end at 16:8 and they had to make sense of the Gospel on that basis. The point is reinforced by the modern versions of the New Testament which print Mark 16:9–20 as a footnote (early edition of the RSV) or an appendix (NIV, TEV): what will a new generation of readers make of Mark? Thus, in spite of the theories of a lost ending, the problem which this study addresses still stands: on the basis of comparisons with ancient literature and of analysis of the structure and style of Mark, does a text of Mark which ends at 16:8 make sense and, if so, how and what? Fourth, there are a variety and an abundance of critics who see no literary or theological barrier to a conclusion at 16:8.

The scholars who are united in their opinion that 16:1–8 provides a conclusion which is literarily coherent and theologically meaningful are divided in their assessment of how the coherence is accomplished and what the ending means. Involved are the theological and literary motives of the author in recording what is recorded and omitting what is omitted. A related consideration is the impact on the readers, the impact of the ending that is there and the ending that is not there.

One explanation suggests that the author has some overriding program other than the resurrection, that Mark is shifting the attention of the readers by omitting the appearances. Mark may, for instance, be looking past the resurrection to the parousia, the return of the risen Lord (Perrin, 1970:26). Mark 13 demonstrates the author's keen interest in that subject and the angelic testimony of 16:7 may point to the promise of parousia, but the parousia is also absent from the text. This theory still does not explain why the author would have made an unnarrated event the focus of his book or how he would have accomplished it. Another theory is that Mark is deflecting the reader's attention from the resurrection back towards the passion, the events surrounding the crucifixion (Achtemeier: 99; cp. also Bowman). The passion is central for Mark; but the resurrection is as prominent in the prediction passages as the crucifixion. It must still be determined if the omission of the narration of an event necessarily removes emphasis from that event. A related suggestion is that the empty tomb story with which Mark closes his Gospel is actually a translation narrative from an early ascent tradition (Talbert: 42, 52). But however convincing this argument may be, it does not account for the possibility or purpose of such an abrupt ending.

The supposed shift in theological emphasis may have involved the reaction to doctrinal heresy which Mark felt bound to counter. Perhaps Mark invented the empty tomb story and omitted the appearance accounts to refute the *theios-aner* proponents who claimed that the risen Lord had appeared to them as he had the apostles (Weeden, 1971:101f). Perhaps Mark reflects an anti-Jewish-Christian, anti-Jerusalem, anti-disciple bias; this would explain, some suggest, the failure of the women to obey the angel's words and the failure of the disciples to follow Jesus to Galilee.[16] But this fascinating theological interpretation rests on a literary assumption—that an event (such as the report of the women or the reunion of the disciples) which is unnarrated does not occur in the mind of the readers. The pages that follow will test that assumption.

The function of the concepts of fear and silence in the final verses of Mark is another area where disagreement remains among those who accept 16:8 as the legitimate conclusion.[17] Is the fear of the women reverential awe which motivated them to obedience or abject terror which blocked further action? Is their silence the surest sign of their failure to carry out the angelic instructions or the appropriate prelude to obedient proclamation? Those who simply assert that fear and silence must have been followed by faith and proclamation have not always based their assumptions on sound internal evidence from the structure of the Gospel of Mark. Those who claim that fear and silence are indications of failure and faithlessness may have overlooked the structural role which those concepts play in Marcan miracle stories. The succeeding chapters will test these assumptions by means of a careful structural analysis.

Some scholars have insisted that the abrupt conclusion of Mark is not to be explained on theological grounds at all; literary factors account for the sharp curtailment. The author—his intentions and expertise—is one literary factor.[18] Is he an unpolished writer who

[16] See discussions by Weeden (1971), Kelber (1979), Tyson (1961), and Crossan (1978) for the failure motif.

[17] Bibliographic entries by Lightfoot, Lane, Moule, Kümmel, Boomershine, and Tyson discuss the fear/silence issue. See more recently Goulder (1978:235–240), and Culpepper (1978:596–597).

[18] Culpepper (1978:596–596) and Bowman (1965) make the same point. See also Lightfoot (1950:95) and Weeden (1971:46).

does not know how to end a narrative or a skillful impressionistic writer adept at suggestion and surprise? Both opinions have been expressed. Is he following a long-standing practice of narrating a promise but not its fulfillment or is he inventing a device, unbound by (or ignorant of) literary convention? Again both interpretations have been suggested. The narrative strategy of Mark must be explored more fully.

Apart from the matter of literary devices lies the issue of authorial silence. "Mark brings his gospel to an end on a high note of enforced terror and puts down his pen because the rest is silence, and cannot be told" (Evans: 68). What does it mean when an author falls silent before the reader is finished listening? Does he know no more? Is he afraid to reveal the rest? Or does he expect the reader to "read on," to respond to the silence by supplying the unnarrated conclusion on the basis of what has been narrated? This last suggestion is more and more common among Mark's commentators (e.g., Petersen, 1980; Williamson, 1983; and Best, 1983); but the theory needs to be supported by recent investigations into the phenomenon of readerly response. The next chapter addresses that fundamental issue.

In spite of the suggestiveness and even the likelihood of many of the interpretations of the ending of Mark which we have surveyed, there remains a certain dissatisfaction. There is something unsatisfying about the attempts to imagine or manufacture an original literary ending to fill in the ending that is not there; they ignore the primitive textual form of the Gospel and the powerful if ambiguous impact of the truncated ending on modern readers. And yet many readers are uneasy with the attempts to support closure at 16:8 by interjecting a theological program into the presumed purpose of Mark which substitutes parousia for resurrection and depends on an imagined theological controversy. This approach also fails, in a way, to take the ending at face value. What if Mark means what he says? What if the ending is intended to focus on Jesus rather than the women or the disciples? What if the resurrection of Jesus is the point and not the empty tomb or the absence of Jesus or the return of Jesus? Then why does Mark say what he says in the way that he says it? Or, we should say, why does Mark say what he says in the way he does not say it? Perhaps that is the real question, the narrator's silence rather than the women's silence, the literary absence of the post-resurrection account rather than the theological absence of the risen Lord. If so, then the problem is not so much the identification of the theological controversy behind the Gospel but the understanding of the literary closure within it. At least the theological freight which the ending carries must be analyzed in the light of the literary function of that ending.

Closure is not simply the way a work ends; it is the "sense of a literary ending derived from the satisfaction of textually generated expectations" (Petersen: 152). So what we sense depends as much on what we expect as on what is stated; and what we expect depends on how the author prepares us by and in the whole narrative. In other words, the ending of Mark may well be about the resurrection of Jesus and his appearance to his followers, even though it does not narrate either.

This study, then, pursues a decidedly literary line of investigation based on the hypothesis that Mark affirms and communicates a resurrection and post-resurrection reunion without narrating them. We will focus on and attempt to delineate an ending which is not there, not the absent, not the omitted, not the lost ending, but the suspended ending of Mark.

CHAPTER II

"THE PROMIS'D END":
THE THEORY OF ABSENT ENDINGS

> Of course, not everything is unsayable in words, only the living truth.
>
> —Ionesco[1]

One of the more intriguing of the many ironies of language is that "words do not signify the presence of things but their absence. Verbalization changes the nature of psychic activities and indicates its absence; it does not change the nature of the material objects but establishes their absence rather than their presence" (Todorov: 101–102). The complementary truth is that "the lack of a sign can itself be a sign" (Merleau-Ponty: 73). This double irony suggests that language and meaning are more complex than they appear and that at the heart of the irony is the signifying power of silence.

The phenomenon has been described in various ways. Kermode (1979:2) emphasizes the superiority of "latent sense" over "manifest sense" in written communication. Polanyi (1967:24) insists that, when we read, "all the time we are guided by sensing the presence of a hidden reality. . . ." Iser (1978:225) points to a work's "blanks and negations" which "denote the missing links and the virtual themes along the syntagmatic and paradigmatic axes of the text." Whatever the terminology, the point is that "language can never explicitly state the meaning" and "meaning emerges as the reverse side of what the text has depicted" (Iser: 228–229).

This "indirect and allusive" (Funk, 1966:224) quality of language produces what might be called the euphemistic phenomenon—the process of indicating an object or conveying a meaning "not by naming it but by avoiding the name" (Schneidau: 268). It explains the power of the metaphor which is not simply the combination of

---

[1] Ionesco is quoted in Steiner: 52.

words which point to or parallel each other but a space, a tension, a force between two words which are askew. Pascal (1952:297) long ago recognized that a skewed space, a pregnant silence, is at the heart of metaphorical language; in his simply profound way he explained that "a type conveys both absence and presence, pleasure and pain."

Linguistics has bequeathed to literary studies a valuable insight: "in the study of language in a social perspective we need both to pay attention to what is said and at the same time to relate it systematically to what might have been said but was not" (Halliday: 59). The insight has far-reaching consequences. A metaphor simply makes explicit the tension that is in every word, and a sentence simply makes explicit the story that is in every metaphor. No level of language or aspect of literature is immune to the pervasive power of the absent. "Rhythm, formal structure, symbol, and the world-creating structure of language are themselves rooted in silence" (Davis: 82).

Modern literary theorists have not altogether ignored the issue of significant silence in literature. In fact, two influential if very different modern schools of criticism have made the explication of the latent their primary goal. For Heidegger, a founding and formidable proponent of phenomenology, the task of that analytical approach is "to let something that lies hidden be seen, that hidden something which really constitutes the meaning and ground of the phenomenon"; in other words, its goal is to show "what is said in the text but not in its words" (Via: 13–14). Ricoeur has defined structuralism as "a kind of asceticism, or if you prefer, a sort of mysticism—the devaluation of the dominant meaning, the renunciation of the dominant in order to yield to something like the presence of an absence" (Leon-Dufour: 101). While these schools of criticism study absence as an underlying characteristic of the texts themselves, other critics emphasize the effects of textual gaps on the reader.

Although the devices for creating meaningful gaps in texts are numerous, there is one over-arching reason for their creation and careful analysis: according to Wayne Booth, they require "a secret communion of the author and reader." Booth (1961:300–304) delineates three varieties of this communion. Some novels appeal to the pleasure of "deciphering," a sense of involvement in the plot and its outcome; other novels encourage a sense of "collaboration," forcing the reader to a higher level of alertness. Still other novels which employ gaps, confusions, and ambiguity demand an act of "collusion": "Whenever an author conveys to his reader an unspoken point, he creates a sense of collusion against all those, whether in the story or out of it, who do not get the point." Elizabeth Bowen (1958:1), herself a practitioner of the art of exclusion (the eloquent omission of a word, a phrase, a paragraph, or a chapter which the reader nonetheless experiences), uses similar language. "In acting upon us, the story is drawing upon us, our responses must contribute; our contributions create. . . .The reality (for us) of the story is a matter of how much it has elicited from us. We enter in, and through this entering in know ourselves to be active. We cooperate." Polanyi stresses the heuristic function of the unspoken in literature: "when a discovery solves a problem, it is itself fraught with further intimations of an indeterminable range." In other words, literature which expresses more than it says demands an act of finding which forces readers into a future of which the text is the foundation but they themselves are the builders. "Furthermore," Polanyi (1967:23) claims, "when we accept the discovery as true, we commit ourselves to a belief in all those as yet undisclosed, perhaps as yet unthinkable, consequences." Sensing the unspoken is an act of finding and the act of finding is an act of faith.

As clearly as these critics focus on the central effect of literature which excludes material and leaves gaps, it is Wolfgang Iser who has explored the topic most thoroughly.[2] One of the most significant aspects of his analysis is that he deals not only with novels which used confusion or exclusion as a deliberate device or left significant gaps as a conscious artifice; rather he is dealing with characteristics of literary communication and with characteristic responses. Iser (1978: 168–169) summarizes this nature of communication and the natural response: "Communication in literature . . . is a process set in motion and regulated not by a given code but by a naturally restrictive and magnifying interaction between the explicit and the implicit, between revelation and concealment. What is concealed spurs the reader to action, but this action is also controlled by what is revealed; the explicit in its turn is transformed when the implicit has been brought to light." The points of concealment, the loci of the implicit, Iser (1978:19, 195, 225) calls "blanks" ("formulated omissions," "suspension of connectibility") and "negations" ("unformulated cancellation of expectation"): each is a kind of gap in the text

---

[2] For related approaches to "reader-response" criticism, see Bleich (1981), and Mailloux (1982).

which makes room for the reader, room to act. The effect of the blank is to "stimulate the reader's imaginative activity," to act as a "vital propellant," to "initiate an interaction whereby the hollow form of the text is filled out by the mental images of the reader."

The process is not inevitably successful. Communication necessitates a constant filling of gaps with the reader's projections: but when the blanks are filled exclusively with the reader's own projections, failure results. Only when readers allow the text to inform and modify their projections is there a successful relationship between text and reader, genuine communication" (Iser: 167). At the same time the indeterminacies of the text can only stimulate the reader to action and involvement; they cannot demand" (Iser: 177). Still, the goal of the writer is to utilize the natural and contrived asymmetries, contingencies, and indeterminacies of a text to prompt interaction, just as the goal of an advertiser is to employ a slogan or song to elicit from the listener the unspoken name of a product. The key is expectation, the "expectation of good continuance." When any blank or break nullifies that expectation of good continuance, "the imagination is automatically mobilized, thus increasing the constitutive activity of the reader, who cannot help but try and supply the missing links that will bring the schemata together in an integrated gestalt" (Iser: 186).

The Sense of the Ending

Just as recent criticism has given considerable attention to the silent spaces in language, so have modern critics shown interest in the way literary works do or do not end.

"Is this the promis'd end?" So asks Kent upon seeing Lear carrying Cordelia's body in his arms (*King Lear* V.III). We sense what he means by "end": it is the end of Cordelia, an end for Lear, for the family, the end of a whole series of events. And we sense what he means by "promis'd"; Kent wants to know if things were bound to end this way, if he should have expected them to turn out like this. Once again, the key to our sense of an ending is our expectation of it. Frank Kermode (1967:17) has forcibly drawn our attention to this phenomenon. In life, we "make considerable imaginative investment in coherent patterns which, by the provision of an end, make possible a satisfying consonance with the origins and with the middle." In literature, we also seek coherence; we expect a conclusion, a point, a punch line. In fact, stories or jokes which disregard the conventions of closure demonstrate their and our dependence on the "sense" of an ending (Kermode, 1979:53).

Kermode's emphasis is shared by Paul Ricoeur. He (1975:46) suggests that in the process of reading we are all the while reading both toward an end and back toward the beginning, "reading the end in the beginning and the beginning in the end." It is a process he calls "followability": "The reader proceeds forward under the thrust of expectation to the conclusion which provides a vantage point from which the story is seen as a whole."[3] Plot—the ingredient which transforms an open-ended series of events into a configuration, a story—makes possible and at the same time depends on this sense of an ending. In spite of the fact that plot involves *peripeteia* (reversal) as well as order, Ricoeur (1974:44, 48–49) can confidently state that "in all story-telling some order finally prevails." Indeed, *peripeteia* ("the falsification of our expectation of the end") is effective precisely because of the readers' confidence in the end, coupled with their desire to reach that end "by an unexpected and instructive route" (Kermode, 1967:18).

But the language of Kermode and Ricoeur implies that the end itself is not as certain as our sense of it. Several points stand out. First, our endings are ever "provisional," a looking forward, a projection on the basis of a pattern. Second, the significance of our sense of an ending is illustrated by those stories which do not end as expected or those jokes which do not end at all. Third, even endings which appear to achieve full literary closure cannot bring their stories to a complete halt nor can they curtail completely readerly activity: they often function as new middles, turning points from which the readers retrace their steps through the text to its beginning. An intriguing picture begins to emerge; it can be stated in three propositions:

1) that the specific sense we have of endings is based on expectation, the expectation of an ending;

2) that the endings we read or sense are both endings and beginnings of the on-going but unnarrated story or of our re-reading of the fore-going story; and

3) that endings which by some device or another have been suspended from the text, absent endings, may communicate as

---

[3] Ricoeur (1975:44) borrows the term from W. B. Gallie's analysis of how historians make history comprehensible.

meaningfully as those which include complete denouement. Each of these propositions will inform the investigations which comprise this study. The point which is most germane to the analysis of the ending of Mark and which demands a further word from a theoretical point of view is the sense of the absent or suspended ending.

The Sense of the Absent Ending

Novelists and critics alike have stressed effective conclusions. Well into this century full closure was taught, practiced, and evaluated as the ideal. But closure has always been an illusory, if necessary, element of narrative literature. "The narratable inherently lacks finality" (Miller: xi). Every story tends to continue; every attempt to cut it off is artificial at best and awkward at worst. Even the classic closural formula, "And they all lived happily ever after," is not only an end but a new beginning—the beginning of life together in the case of the prince and princess or of reunited lives in the case of the separated family. This ending deliberately opens up the future, an on-going, unending, "ever after" future. Not only do we know that there is an "after"; we know its quality, its character—it is happy. The so-called ending is a summary of, a substitute for, the rest of the story. Fulfillment, the complement of expectation, is achieved by what is narrated about what is not narrated.

It is not that stories, novels, and other narratives do not build toward closure—Kermode has already convincingly demonstrated the strong impulse for resolution, coherence, and consonance—it is just that the effort is never complete or absolute (Miller: xiv). Closure never completely conquers the momentum of narrative. In most cases there is closure of a sort; consonance is attained; a satisfactory resolution is achieved. Even the traditional novel, with its significant investment in narrative closure, must make at least a "token gesture to imply that there may be more to tell." Roland Barthes calls this characteristic the "pensivity" of the novel (Miller: 274). But it is the modern novel which has not only recognized the inevitability of the ending which does not end but has also exploited the power of the absent ending.

Experience is open and opens onto other experiences. Narrative is by nature open, unclosed and unclosable. The modern acceptance of these statements has predetermined a species of fiction which is open and open-ended. Alan Friedman has traced the evolution of this form and has analyzed its use. For the purpose of this study the development is not as important as the phenomenon itself.

> Can we say that final episodes which might in the past have
> delineated a containing reorganization of experience, no
> longer do so. . . ? To put it that way would not, of course, be
> to say that there are no final episodes, still less that there is
> never any reorganization of experience. It would be to say
> clearly that final episodes of reorganization (specifically) are
> simply absent; or else that the specific reorganization of
> experience which is delineated is finally one that holds the
> previous mounting disturbance at an unreduced or even
> slightly intensified pitch (1966:30).

Novels, of course, still come to an end but they do so in such a way
that the action is unchecked or even expanding. The modern novel-
ist E. M. Forster (1927:169) bears witness to this tendency.

> Expansion. That is the idea the novelist must cling to. Not
> completion. Not rounding off but opening out. When the
> symphony is over we feel that the notes and tunes . . . have
> been liberated, they have found in the rhythm of the whole
> their individual freedom. Cannot the novel be like that? Is
> there not something of it in *War and Peace?* Such an untidy
> book. Yet as we read it, do not great chords begin to sound
> behind us, and when we have finished does not every item
> . . . lead a larger existence than was possible at the time?

Friedman (1966:xiii) sees this yearning as a particularly modern one,
akin to the modern vision of endlessness and unlimited experience.

Wayne Booth (1961:287) has focused on a somewhat darker side
of the phenomenon—the deliberate confusion of the reader in regard to the plot, the outcome, even the truth. The ambiguous and
equivocal nature of the text leaves the reader "baffled," "discon-
certed," even "staggered". This effect is especially noticeable in the
literature of the moral quest where an end, a result, a right result, is
expected. It is not unusual for the modern novel to end with hero
and reader lost, the quest unfulfilled, and more questions raised
than answered. What Booth (1961:297) prophesied on the basis of
the literature he analyzed has come to pass: "One can theoretically
project a novel in which no attempt would be made to give a sense of
projection toward any conclusion or final illumination." In fulfilling
Booth's prediction, anti-literature employs silence and the sense of
absence with a vengeance: its open structure of meanings includes
"a major unresolved conflict with the intent of displaying its unre-
solvedness" (Hassan: 1967). In the process, novels like those of Alain
Robbe-Grillet question not only the possibility of coherent con-

clusion, but the possibility of language, literature, meaning, and civilization.[4]

What emerges in those narratives which try to end but cannot, as well as those which consciously employ open-endedness and exploit it, is a sense of the potential impact of the ending that does not end. There is power in the improbability of such a conclusion. A linguistic principle which is likewise true of literature is that "the less probable a particular element is, the more meaning it has in that context ('element' should here be taken to refer to all the results of 'choice', including . . .)" (Lyons: 415). Our familiarity with the norms of language (whether these norms are really characteristic of the essence of language or not) causes a reaction to any deviation from those norms: the greater the deviation, the greater the impact. There is also power in the very absence of a conclusion. It may be a literal absence of words or an absence in which the words present point to an unwritten sense. Variations of the sentence "He is a lion" illustrate the point (Rabkin: 18). If by "lion" we mean literally a lion, we have already created suspense by syntactically postponing the word until the end of the sentence. If we mean a brave person, we have substituted a metaphorical connotation which nonetheless derives its impact from the unspoken literal meaning. If we mean a coward, we have substituted an ironic connotation which depends on the absent but implicit connotation of a real lion. Of course, the sentence "He is a real _____" interferes most radically with the process by forcing the reader or listener to fill in the slot. The point is, by a variety of means, some blatant, some subtle, the act of not finishing a sentence straightforwardly or at all intensifies the process of communication. Thus the suspended ending is doubly powerful by virtue of the reverberating silence itself and the surprise attached to it.

The dynamic of the suspended ending is further demonstrated by the residual effect it produces. Rabkin (1973: 121) defines narrative residue as "that which remains after a comparison or bisociation, and implies a continuing diachronic structure." All literature has some residual effect; every form from folktales to poems to sermons has been used at times to communicate cultural norms, noble thoughts, or theological verities. But we are talking about more than the didactic function of literature. We mean a feature of

---

[4] See *Topology of a Phantom City, Jealousy, In the Labyrinth, The Erasers,* and Robee-Grillet's critical work *For a New Novel.*

narrative itself, this residue, which carries us forward within a text. "We do not wait to see what the ending will be; our perception of the structure in the central metaphor tells us that. We wait to see how it comes out as we know it must" (Rabkin: 125). This, as Iser and Kermode and Ricoeur have pointed out, is the way we read: "we have metaphor within metaphor; . . . structures are begun and their completion is suspended while other structures are begun and the subliminal suspense keeps us going until the comparison made is multiplied by the device" (Rabkin: 44). And this is what engages the reader in the style of the story.

The next step is to recognize that this residual effect is even greater and the engagement with the story's style is stronger when the suspended structure is the ending. In this case the reader is carried forward not within the text but within the story which the text tried to bring to a close but did not, the story which the reader must try to end in consonance with the total structure of the story. This suspension "keeps us going" as a space probe keeps going. Against the resistance of mass and matter the booster gives the ship its thrust and trajectory; once past the atmosphere, once past the magnetic field of the earth, once out into the void, the ship does not end its journey for lack of resistance but continues along the same trajectory now unencumbered by the confines of gravity and friction. So the story is launched by the text and, not ending its journey at the outer limits of the text, it continues unabated when it reaches the silence at the end of the text. When the conclusion of the story occurs not under the restraining influence of the friction of the language of the text but in the expanding space of the reader's mind, its impact is intensified.

The obvious example is Stockton's "The Lady or the Tiger," a story whose structure is centered on a choice. Building anticipation regarding that choice provides the suspense. But many stories are suspenseful; what makes this story uniquely compelling is not its suspensefulness but its suspended ending. What interests us at this point is not merely the absent ending but its dynamic effect and the way it achieves that effect. In "The Lady or the Tiger"

> the withholding of the answer functions to make the very decision a metaphor for justice and for life. It adds something that is in keeping with what has been going on all along: the metaphorization of the unknowable in life. We see then that, although plot-suspense asks for an answer, the presence of that answer is not what makes a story good.

> What is essential is that a certain kind of necessity be
> fulfilled . . . (Rabkin: 64–65).

In this case, the fulfillment comes through silence, by means of an absence, a suspended ending.

Rabkin's formulation of the residual effect of metaphorical silence is important for the way it brings together the effect of expectation, suspense, textual silences, and absent but significant conclusions. But Kermode (1979:65) provides our thesis: "we can derive the sense of fulfilled expectation, of satisfactory closure, from texts that actually do not provide what we ask, but give us instead something that, out of pure desire for completion, we are prepared to regard as a metaphor or synecdoche for the ending that is not there." This insight forms the theoretical core of this study and is, as supported by the ideas we have surveyed, the cornerstone of a positive literary interpretation of the truncated ending of the Gospel of Mark. But the leap from twentieth century literary theory to first century gospel is an abrupt one. Only if these principles are clearly present in the ancient literary context of which Mark was a part can we confidently claim that our assessment of Mark's suspended ending is anything other than a modern imposition on an ancient text. Once we have determined that ancient writers, including Biblical writers, communicated by means of similar devices, we can analyze the use of those literary devices in Mark in the search for a solution to the problem of the meaning of its ending.

CHAPTER III

"WHEN TO BE SILENT": SUSPENDED ENDINGS IN ANCIENT LITERATURE

> Socrates. Is there not another kind of word or speech far better than this, and having far greater power . . . ? I mean an intelligent word graven in the soul of the learner, which can defend itself, and knows when to speak and when to be silent.
>
> —PLATO (*Phaedrus* 275–276)

The Rhetoric of Silence in Ancient Literary Criticism

> A whole is that which has a beginning, a middle, and an end. A beginning is that which does not itself follow anything by causal necessity, but after which something naturally is or comes to be. An end, on the contrary, is that which itself naturally follows some other thing, either by necessity, or as a rule, but has nothing following it. A middle is that which follows something as some other thing follows it. A well-constructed plot, therefore, must neither begin nor end at haphazard, but conform to these principles (*Poetics* VII.3).

Aristotle's dictum is notable for its concise view of the structure of plot, especially its emphasis on the beginning and the end. It is also notable for the frequency with which it is violated. The violations stem not from the fact that Aristotle was in error about the nature of plot or the importance of structure but from the fact that plot and story are not coterminous. For example, the well-constructed plot of the *Iliad* begins in the midst of the story of the Trojan war; the Greeks have landed, built defenses, and engaged in battle over nine years. The well-rounded plot climaxes with the story unended: the Trojans hold Troy, the Greeks are on the shore still far from home, the war continues. Even the more personal story of Achilles stretches back before the plot to indispensible exploits and forward past the end of the plot to his death. The *Iliad* begins and ends *in medias res;* the past which stretches out behind the beginning and future which forges on from the end are absent but haunting presences. The beginning is powerful because we know what follows. This insight does not contradict Aristotle's view; his emphasis on the beginning and the end underlies our ability to study variations in how texts do or do not end. But the example of the *Iliad* does support the complex relation of plot and story, the sophistication with which ancient storytellers could set forth their plots, and more specifically the ability of an author to bring a "well-constructed plot" to a conclusion without closing off the action of the story. These open endings—silent about but signifying the future—and other gaps and silences, did not go unnoticed by ancient rhetoricians.

Demetrius, a fourth century contemporary of Aristotle, recognized the power of the implicit: "often the indirect [*plagion* = oblique] expression is more impressive than the direct" (Demetrius: 199–120). But he was especially conscious of the significance of the silent. His term—and the usage was followed by later rhetoricians—for the figure of speech was *aposiopesis,* which he described as a "sudden reticence," "a suppressed clause," the "figure of silence" (Demetrius: 268). From his rhetorical viewpoint the effect of the figure was all important. Like praetermission or praeterition (mentioning a fact while implying it is not being mentioned, using a phrase like "not to mention . . . ," or "I shall pass over . . . "), *aposiopesis* (not mentioning a fact while assuming that it has been mentioned) "will also make expression more forcible" (Demetrius: 189). "In certain cases conciseness and especially silence *(aposiopesis)* produce elevation, since some things seem to be more significant when not expressed but hinted at" (Demetrius: 119). Again with an illustration, Demetrius asserted that, "a sudden lapse into silence is often yet more forcible as Demosthenes says, 'I could on my part . . . but I do not desire to say anything so offensive. . . .' The orator's reserve [*ho siopesas*] in not saying what he "could on his part" have said is more effective than any possible retort could have been" (Demetrius: 141, 185).

Several rhetoricians who flourished in the first century B.C. were also interested in the effects of literary silence. Dionysius of Halicarnassus made many references to the effective use of pauses *(siope),* delays, stops, obstructions and abridgments. These silences which stand for what is not there, he said give emphasis to what is there. Horace (65–8 B.C.), the Roman "literary critic" who emphasized self-consistency of character and plot within a narrative, also spoke to the matter of unacted scenes and unnarrated action. After asserting that "less vividly is the mind stirred by what finds entrance through the ears than by what is brought before the trusty eyes," Horace expressed a modifying opinion. "Yet you will not bring upon the stage what would be performed behind the scenes, and you will keep much from our eyes, which an actor's ready tongue will narrate anon in our presence, so that Medea is not to butcher her boys before the people, nor impious Atreus cook human flesh upon the stage, nor Procne be turned into a bird, Cadmus into a snake. Whatever you thus shew me, I discredit and abhor" (Horace: 465). We know that Horace thought some dramatic climaxes should be suspended. We are less certain of his reasons. Were such endings too gruesome for human sensibilities? Were they too impossible for dramatic practicality? Or did they have greater impact and effect unstaged than staged? Whatever our conclusion, Horace recognized that at times omission served the purpose of dramatic consistency.

The Roman rhetorician Quintilian (c . A.D. 35-c. 96) was still interested in the power of omission as late as the end of the first century A.D.[1] Referring to a variety of related figures including synecdoche and aposiopesis, Quintilian recognized that they could be utilized for a variety of purposes: to achieve novelty, brevity, a sense of decency, a sense of vivaciousness, vehemence, energy, or passion. He drew a fine distinction between aposiopesis and synecdoche which does not necessarily relate to their usage by other ancient or modern critics. Aposiopesis is a suppressed uncertainty while synecdoche is the omission of anything easily understood from the rest. By a strategic reticence or interruption aposiopesis communicates a passion more than a verbal expression. The *Aeneid* supplies an example:

> Do you really dare, you Winds, without my divine consent
> To confound earth and sky, and raise this riot of water?
> You, whom I—well, you have made the storm, I must lay it.

Synecdoche occurs when "from a thing actually expressed another may be understood" (VIII.6.22). Thus the lines

---

[1] The most obvious references include Quintilian *Institutes of Oratory* VIII.6.22; IX.2.54–57; IX.3.50–58.

> Behold the oxen homeward bring their ploughs
> Suspended from the yoke

simply but evocatively communicate the coming of night. In both cases the suspended expression creates an added emphasis and elicits added reader involvement.

Another piece of criticism dating from the first Christian century, "Longinus" *On the Sublime* speaks of the "wonder and transport" (I.4) which result from the experience of the unspoken. "And so even without being spoken the bare idea often of itself wins admiration for its inherent genius. How grand, for instance, is the silence of Ajax in the Summoning of the Ghosts, more sublime than any speech" (IX.2). This critical comment must serve as a final reminder that ancient rhetoricians sensed the significance of silence, even in climactic dramatic moments; it also suggests, by its reference to the *Odyssey*, that in ancient narratives themselves we can find the testing ground for our theory of suspended endings and the training ground for reading the suspended ending of Mark intelligently.

Suspended Endings in Ancient Epics

"The typical epic, though it must have a close, does not have an end . . . and instinctively the supreme epic poets close their work in such a way as to leave us with a vivid sense of *going-on*" (Duckworth: 28).

Homer's *Iliad* and *Odyssey* and Vergil's *Aeneid* serve as sources for the testing of this principle. These epics became the standards and sources of Greco-Roman literature and were universally known in the Hellenistic world. So, although far different from a gospel generically, their conclusions can be compared profitably to that of Mark, another ancient narrative which closes without ending.

The Iliad. As with the Gospel of Mark, a textual problem clouds the issue of the conclusion of the *Iliad*. According to many Homeric critics, Books XXIII and XXIV, "the last books, which form a noble sequel to the poem, are in all probability later works . . . " (Browne: 109). It is not so unlikely that a later author (out of reverence not irreverence to the genius of Homer) would have attempted this "noble sequel." What we know as the Epic Cycle is a series of later works which attempt to fill in the gaps in the Homeric epics. The *Cypria* chronicles from the decision of the gods to cause the war up to the quarrel. The *Little Iliad* takes us from the death of Achilles to the fall of Troy. And the *Sack of Ilion* retraces the events from the building of the wooden horse through the city's fall (Lattimore: 24).

If some analysts are correct—if the last two books are another in a series of attempts to bring closure to strands of the complex story of the *Iliad*—the narration of the mourning over Patroclus, his funeral and burial, and the ceremonial games in his honor are no part of the epic text. Neither are the dragging of Hector's body, the poignant meeting of Achilles and Priam, and the emotions and events surrounding the burial of Hector. Instead, the epic ends with the slaying of Hector by Achilles and the grief of Hecuba, Priam, and Andromache. The poet leaves Patroclus and Hector dead and disgraced; very little seems resolved except the personal destinies of two adversaries. According to this theory, the *Iliad* ends with the mourning of Andromache: "So she spoke, in tears; and the women joined in her mourning."

The very existence of a sequel—if it is an addition—forms the basis for several important assumptions:

1) that the ending, by pointing to the future (the imagined fate of Hector's fatherless son) encourages speculation about what happened next;

2) that the ending is open enough to allow attempts at closure;

3) that the tradition offered the general parameters within which any projections could be suitably made;

4) that the text supplied sufficient anticipatory clues about future events that later readers/poets could supplement the narrative in a way that convinced succeeding generations of its originality and authenticity; and

5) that readers of the truncated original no doubt adequately supplied the necessary resolutions, given the demands of the text and the demands of custom, even before the attachment of the sequel.

On the other hand, there is no certainty that the *Iliad* closed with Book XXII. The stylistic differences which suggested the problem to some critics have not convinced most commentators or editors. Assuming that the *Iliad* was composed as it stands, including Books XXIII and XXIV, and ignoring the textual problem altogether, we are still left with a conclusion which leaves unnarrated the very events the work itself led us to anticipate.

Erich Auerbach's (1953:3–23) celebrated foreground/background distinction is only part of the story. There is the fully externalized style which Homer used to such powerful effect in the "leisurely digressions of ample detail," but there is another style, an "allusive, elliptical" style, used to refer to some of the most essential elements of the story's background (Austin: 71–72).

> There is in Homer a principle which might be called one of oblique concentration. To praise Achilleus Homer describes his shield. . . . There is a certain direct simplicity in the narrative which hides the obliquity of the style, the style which marks the important by evading the explicit statement and glances instead on all the circumferential details (Austin: 80).

In fact much of the key background material, known even by modern readers and unthinkingly read into the text throughout, is omitted or presented in the scantiest allusions (Austin: 72; Lattimore: 23–24). There is an oblique reference to the "judgment" of Paris, the fateful decision which raised the ire of rival goddesses in XXIV.25–30; but there is only silence when Zeus directly asks Hera the cause of their strife (IV.31–33). The abduction of Helen—the incident which launched not only ships but a long costly war—is vaguely alluded to in III.39–57. That the Achaian heroes were Helen's former suitors who were now bound to stand by Menelaus, the one who won her hand, is never mentioned. Neither do we learn of Iphigenia's sacrificial death which permitted the stalled expedition to sail on to Troy.

The suspension of incidents foreshadowed in the *Iliad* and therefore expected by its listeners by virtue of common knowledge as well as textual innuendo is even more notable. On the personal level, the choice Achilles makes of a short but glorious life is basic to the plot; his death ever looms in the near future. In fact, his death is foreshadowed (XVIII.95–125, XXII.359–360). There is even a vague hint at the vulnerability of his heel in XXII.395–398. But his death is not narrated. On the political level, the outcome of the long war, the Achaian victory, and the fall and destruction of Troy, are not related at all even though they are insinuated by the author and assumed by the reader. One of the most famous incidents in the war—the ruse of the Trojan horse—is not even mentioned.

"As Homer says simply, ending this long and complex story, truly without beginning or end. . . ., 'Thus they buried horse-taming Hector'" (Beye: 157). There is no real conclusion in the narrative; but by a number of techniques Homer achieves closure outside the bounds of the epic itself. "In the course of the action, the characters are often made to look forward, beyond the 'end,' in thought and speech" (Hägg: 309). The allusions to Achilles' impending death grow in intensity until, "when the *Iliad* ends, the details of Achilles' death and burial are familiar to the reader" (Duckworth: 28). The ending that is there—Archilles' defeat of Hector—is a synecdoche for the two endings which are not there—the death of Achilles and the fall of Troy. It is in the death of Hector that the clearest prophecy of Achilles' death comes (XX.355–359) and the clue to the means of his death appears (XX.395–398). And it is in the death of Hector that we see microcosmically the fall of his people. "In avenging Patroklos, he saves the Greeks. In killing Hector, he dooms Troy" (Lattimore: 17).

The effect of this device is as crucial as the technique. "The poem ends on a quiet note, the funeral of Hector, but the later events—death of Achilles and the fall of the fated city—have impressed themselves upon the consciousness of the reader almost as vividly as if the poet had extended his epic to include them" (Duckworth: 31). "The fact that the epic closes at the time of Achilles' triumph merely accentuates the pathos which has been built up by the long series of prophecies" (Duckworth: 28). Of Homer's reticence in narrating the dramatic death of Troy, one writer says, "Resounding through the epic, now in styled allusions, now in strident lament, is the dread fact that an ancient and splendid city has perished by the edge of the sea" (Steiner: 174). Thus real beginnings and the real ends are not narrated; the cause of the war, the course of the war, and the outcome of the war are barely mentioned. But by bold allusions they are incorporated into one compact incident—the wrath of Achilles—and are thereby amplified. And "though beginning and ending in the tenth year we have a sense of the beginning and end of the war" (Lattimore: 31).

The Odyssey. "Altogether it must . . . be admitted that the end of the *Odyssey,* to put it bluntly, is bungled. . . ." (Bury: 3). The problem is a matter of style. Critics point to discrepancies in language, variations in meter, and changes in versification. Long recapitulations strike most readers as redundant and completely unnecessary for the understanding of the text. The narrative logic seems altered in the last sections. And different concepts, different treatments of concepts, and contradictory approaches to the same concepts have also been catalogued.

As a result of these stylistic problems, modern and ancient critics alike have identified XXXIII.296 as the last line of the original

Odyssey. Two ancient sources bear testimony to this opinion. "Aristarchus and Aristophanes say that this is the end of the *Odyssey.*" And again elsewhere, "Aristophanes and Aristarchus make this the limit of the *Odyssey*" (Page: 101f). If they were correct, four important episodes—Odysseus' review of his adventures for Penelope, the picture of the suitors in Hades, the reunion of Odysseus and his father Laertes, and the battle between Odysseus and the relatives of the suitors—are omitted. Many modern scholars are convinced that these were not originally part of the text. "We need not argue whether the earlier references to Laertes in the *Odyssey* lead us to expect a meeting between father and son before the end of the poem: it is certain that the meeting described in our *Odyssey* was composed at an era much later than the bulk of the *Odyssey*" (Page: 111). Another critic makes the sweeping claim that "The most severe advocates of unity of authorship from the Alexandrian critics to Monro are forced to admit that. . . . the whole of the last book and part of the twenty-third book of the Odyssey is late work patched on to the end of the poem" (Browne: 135).

But this verdict is by no means universal. An ending which sees Odysseus and Penelope to their bed chamber and closes the door, an ending which omits scenes which have occasioned considerable analysis over the centuries, is not lightly allowed. Some argue that XXXIII.296 is an unsuitable ending: "That the poet could have contemplated the reunion of Odysseus with Penelope as an artistic or even tolerable ending to his poem appears to me almost incredible" (Bury: 5). Others argue that the omitted episodes are essential. Odysseus' summary of his exploits for Penelope was "almost a necessity of Homer's treatment" (Bury: 8). Given contemporary custom and considering narrative foreshadowing, the narration of the reunion of father and son was a requisite, they insist. And commentators claim that the fight between Odysseus and the kinsmen of the dead suitors was essential to satisfy the Greek concept and Homeric theme of justice (Clarke: 78, 85). "It is necessary, for the satisfaction of those who listened to the recitation, to tell how the inevitable feud between Odysseus and the men of Ithaca . . . was composed . . ." (Bury: 6).

Several alternate solutions appeal to those who recognize the stylistic problems in the epic's ending but who are uncomfortable with the opinion of Aristarchus and Aristophanes. Some, of course, maintain that Books XXIII and XXIV are original (Clarke: 85). Others retain the four episodes while explaining the stylistic discrepancies: although Homer died before completing the epic, a less skilled disciple was able to compose the intended conclusion from the notes and outline of the master (Bury: 8). Kirk is sure that the satisfaction of the blood feud would have been narrated and just as certain that the text after XXIII.296 is unhomeric; to resolve the contradiction he posits "some references to the problem" in the original poem which were then "removed in favour of an elaborate and miscellaneous addition" (Kirk: 178). The school of Homeric critics called the Analysts still see the close as a continuation in another hand, a late appendix, added to satisfy the omission of related incidents in the tradition.

This textual problem is interesting in its own right and in comparison with the controversial textual problems in the Greek New Testament. But for the purposes of this study, the question of the ending of the *Odyssey* is secondary to the question of the sense of the ending of the *Odyssey*. Homer's powers may have failed him at the end, a disciple may have bungled his way to the conclusion, or an eager poet may have rounded off Homer's work with his own additions. We know from two parts of the Epic Cycle—*The Returns* and *Telegony*—that later writers were not above "filling in" the gaps they sensed in and after the narrative of the *Odyssey* (Lattimore: 24). The debate will continue. But the debate supplies some interesting information about the way we read endings, specifically suspended endings. In the face of clear, unchallenged, ancient testimony, in the face of strong stylistic evidence, modern critics are swayed by the demands of the expectations created in the text. "There is yet another reason for hestitating to believe that XXIII.296 could have been the end contemplated by Homer. We might expect an intimation that Odysseus told his story to Penelope" (Bury: 7). It is the "serious questions unanswered," like the unresolved blood feud, that worries these scholars; before opting for another solution Kirk (1965:177–178) admits: "it is just conceivable that it was never explicitly resolved; that it was simply assumed that the resourceful Odysseus . . . would easily have overcome the difficulty." Analysts on the other hand must also admit to the power of anticipation before passing their judgment; notice again Page's statement (1955:111): "We need not argue whether references to Laertes in the *Odyssey* lead us to expect a meeting between father and son before the end of the poem. . . ."

As we have seen from the *Iliad*, that these events are fore-shadowed, that they are expected, that we assume them, that they are crucial to the closure of the whole story, is no guarantee that they were originally narrated in the epic poem. Some ancient writer could have felt the demands of the suspended ending and appended his written resolutions just as the author of the *Telegony* did. The point is, the absence of these events is felt as keenly, if not more so, than their presence. If the *Odyssey*'s present shape is original it still leaves many important events foreshadowed but unnarrated. The later life, old age, and death of the hero are alluded to in XI.119–137 and XXIII.286–287, but never related. The vibrancy of those unresolved chords is evident not only in the *Telegony* but centuries later in *The Odyssey: A Modern Sequel* by Kazantzakis. Even the ending that appears to include full closure can only close but not end.

"With happy hearts they came to the place where their old bed was." If this line (XXIII.296) is the end of the epic, Homer has chosen a powerful but understated way to symbolize the reunion of husband and wife as well as the righting of wrongs in Ithaca. The bed—the olive-tree bed, rooted in the soil of Ithaca, shared with his long-separated, long-suffering wife—becomes a symbol, a synecdoche, of reunion and restoration. Like the death of Hector, their happy approach to the old bed silently speaks of long hours of recapitulation, of laughter and tears, and of love. It also speaks of the re-establishment of sovereignty over the land of Ithaca, Ithaca's people, and Ithaca's prize, Penelope, his wife. Whether or not it is the ending, it speaks eloquently of the events we know must follow the hero's return.

The Aeneid. Like the *Iliad* and the *Odyssey*, the ending of the *Aeneid* is problematic. Students of the epic have marvelled at and puzzled at such an abrupt close to such a long and complex work. "Why," one critic asks, "does the epic end so precipitately on this high note of tension?" (Walsh). This "high note of tension" is a private duel in which the epic hero Aeneas slays the native Latin leader Turnus who has just begged for mercy. Invoking the name of Pallas, a comrade whom Turnus had slain and whose spoils Turnus wore, Aeneas

> . . . plunged his sword
> In fury deep into his enemy's heart.
> But as for him his limbs lay slumped and chill
> And his soul flew, resentful of its fate,
> Down to the Shades, with many a sigh and groan (1961: 298).

The work whose avowed purpose is to tell us of the man whose exploits eventuated in the "towers of Rome" (I.1.9) ends with "civilized" Aeneas wreaking vengeance on his vanquished enemy in a private duel. We are reminded of Dorothy Sayer's comment on the close of *The Song of Roland*: "It ends like the *Iliad* and *Aeneid*, in a minor key, and on a falling cadence."

The odd ending has spawned its share of later attempts at more satisfying closure. Other ancient texts narrated events that Vergil had "omitted": the meeting with Dido's sister Anna, Aeneas' purification at the river, and his assumption into heaven.[2] Centuries later in 1428 a young Italian poet rounded off the *Aeneid* by adding a thirteenth book of 630 lines which was published in many subsequent editions of the epic. In this conclusion all the expectations are fulfilled. The Latin army surrenders; Turnus' body is rightfully returned; Aeneas marries the Lavinian princess, makes treaty with her father, lays out the boundaries of the new city, dies, and is transported into the skies (Walsh). Many other attempted additions have followed.

Of course, we have seen enough of the effect of the suspended ending to know that what is at work in the production of these added endings is the power—not the weakness—of the unnarrated conclusion which drives readers to supply the real ending in their own minds if not in their own words. The compulsion under which the later poets labored and the accuracy with which they were able to tie up all the loose ends of the narrative is the greatest proof of the absent presence of that ending in the text. Readers see through the abrupt, almost out-of-character, slaying at the end of the *Aeneid*: and it is for them not a smoky glass, clouded by the petty, almost barbaric, act of a supposedly civilized man, but a telescopic lens which brings a whole future into focus.

The means by which Vergil accomplished this effect were his use of foreshadowing, a suggestive beginning, and a symbolic ending. The beginning of the *Aeneid* "not only forecasts the action of the entire poem . . . but it also looks ahead to the events which lie outside the action of the poem—the founding of Alba Longa and of Rome."[3] In other words, when we read the beginning in the end and the end in the beginning, we are not disappointed that the end does not satisfy our expectations; rather our expectations satisfy (fill out) and interpret the end. The events which are omitted from the conclusion—Aeneas' marriage, peace with the Latins, a new language, a new race, a new city—are so carefully foreshadowed that

[2] Ovid *Metamorphosis* 14.581f; also see *Oxford Classical Dictionary* (1949:12).

[3] Duckworth: 7; note also the interesting lexical bridge between beginning and end formed by the use of the word *condo* in I.5 ("found a city") and XII.950 ("bury").

we read them in the ending even though they remain unwritten (Duckworth: 34). And the suspended ending itself has its intended effect.

> The work ends not in Vergil's own time but in a past just about to change into the epoch of Roman ascendancy. The last bit of the plot is the death of Turnus, which removes the last barrier to the fulfillment of Rome's destiny. This has a strong residual effect, and must have had an even stronger residual effect on the Augustan audience. The finished work, like the moralizing of the folktale, has an educating potential which comes from its structure (Rabkin: 102).

Thus the scene between Aeneas and Turnus is a synecdoche, a metaphor, for the ending that is not there in the narrative but that has been fixing itself in the minds of the reader since the opening lines and asserts itself in the silence after the closing lines.

Suspended Endings in Ancient Tragedy

Greek drama provides another perspective on the question of narrative endings. In these plays the relationship between what is narrated and what is expected but not narrated is supplemented by the relationship between what is staged and what is not staged but only announced. The Chorus and messengers emerge as key factors in communicating these implied but unseen actions. Some ancient tragedies appear to achieve full closure, but many employ the device of suspension in emphasizing the expected climax. The plays of Sophocles tend to represent the closed narrative of collective experience; in *Oedipus the King* most of the conflicts are resolved. Euripides, on the other hand, stressed individual experience and produced plays characterized by a sense of openness; The *Bacchae* "leaves its audience in a state of unreleased anguish" (Hassan: 19). But several plays by both dramatists serve to illustrate the communicative silences, suspended endings, and openness of ancient drama.

Sophocles. A variety of related techniques are employed in the plays of Sophocles. *Oedipus the King* ends with the famous maxim, "Judge no man happy until his whole life has been lived"; the statement looks back to the sad reversals in the King's past but reminds the reader that there is yet more to be told. In *Oedipus at Colonus* the tragic life of the King and the violent events of the play end in quiet mystery as Oedipus dies in a grove known only to

Theseus. The disposition of his body and soul is known to none. The concluding events of *Antigone* are not enacted on stage but are reported in detail by a messenger; the audience "sees" them only through his words. The hero Ajax falls on his sword in plain view of the audience in the play which carries his name; but the final issue—his honorable or dishonorable burial—while resolved in word is not carried out in deed. More significantly, the whole plot of the *Women of Trachis* looks forward to the death of Hercules and his wife Deianira. Deianira dies—off-stage—and the death of Hercules is certain but unnarrated as the play ends. A related dramatic device—foreshadowing a major event which does not take place in the narrative time of the play—appears in Sophocles' *Electra*. From the first speech we know the outcome: Orestes and Electra will avenge their father's death by slaying his murderers, their mother Clytemnestra and Aegisthus. When the play has run its course Clytemnestra has been murdered, again off-stage, but Aegisthus' death has not yet taken place. The play ends with the tyrant being led into the palace to die where he killed Agamemnon.

Three preliminary observations apply by way of summary. First, Sophocles tended to have violent murders take place off-stage, a loud cry and the report of a messenger standing for the action itself. But, second, on-stage deaths were not prohibited as the case of *Ajax* shows. And third, the climactic and concluding event can be predicted, ordered, implied, and then suspended before its dramatization.

Euripides. Three levels of suspension appear in the plays of Euripides. The first is the use of a series of prophecies at the end of the play, forecasting the fates of the major characters. As *Helen* ends we learn that she will become a goddess and Menelaus will pass to the Isle of the Blest. *Orestes, Electra,* and *Andromache* also close with a string of predictions. This device includes the least foreshadowing and anticipation, is least crucial to the plot, and demands the least reader participation. But it is a way of carrying the imagination of the reader beyond the end of the narrative.

The second level involves the substitution of a report about a critical event for the staging of the event itself. In *The Supplicants* the plot hinges on whether or not the people of Argos will harbor the daughters of Danaus and risk war with Egypt. We are assured throughout the play of the hospitality of the Argives and expect a favorable vote. But the decision of the Argive council is not seen on stage; the positive response is relayed later by the King of Argos.

The death of the tyrant Lycus, and of the wife and children of
Hercules, the climaxes of *Hercules Mad*, are not narrated as actions
in the play; a messenger reveals the scene in a subsequent speech.
At the end of *The Trojan Women* Hecuba mournfully describes the
burning of Troy.

Perhaps the most dramatic example of this second level of
suspension comes in Euripides' *Medea*. The impending death of the
children of Jason and Medea dominates the play. It is the focus of
attention in statements by the nurse, the Chorus, and Jason—not to
mention Medea herself. First, the nurse warns: "I am afeared she
may contrive some untoward scheme . . . and I much do dread that
she will plunge the keen sword through their heart." At the very
beginning of the play we are pointed toward the conclusion and told
its content: "the mischief is but now beginning; it has not reached its
climax yet." The certain climax is foreshadowed throughout the play.
At times there is merely an allusion: "I have seen her eyeing them
savagely, as though she were minded to do them some hurt." At
other times the foreshadowing is direct: "for I will slay the children I
have borne." Then again the anticipation comes through ironic
denial: "O my children, since there awaits you even thus a long, long
life. . . ."

Near the end of the play Medea's resolve to slay her children
breaks down briefly: "O, I cannot. . . . No, no, I will not do it." But
only briefly: "I must face this deed." This temporary reversal only
heightens the suspense. But the deed is inevitable: "Die they must
in any case." We do not see presented on stage the death of Creon or
his daughter but the event is described in gory detail. Neither do we
see the climactic event, the inevitable event, the foreshadowed
event, the death of Jason's and Medea's two sons. And, in this case,
in contrast to the description of the earlier murders, there are no
details—no details of the event around which the whole play is built,
toward which the whole play has pointed. We only hear the cries of
the doomed boys when they first realize their mother's intentions.
After that there is only the report by the Chorus, "Thy sons are
dead." Jason wants to see the bodies; the Chorus expects to see the
corpses; and the reader, trusting the Chorus' report of the long-
anticipated but unstaged deed, expects to see the corpses. "Throw
wide the doors and see thy children's murdered corpses," the Chorus cries. "Haste, ye slaves, loose the bolts," Jason commands, "that
I may see the sight of two-fold woe. . . ." But they are not there; the
corpses are beside Medea on an airborne chariot. Jason is not

satisfied; he wants the corpses: "Give up to me those dead, to bury and lament: One last fond kiss, ah me! I fain would on their lips imprint." But he is denied and therein lies the full horror: their deaths known but not seen, their bodies dead but not honored, embraced, even touched, suspended between Hades and Jason's outstretched hands.

The narrative has satisfied the expectations it created. Medea is avenged and Jason is broken. But the satisfaction is accomplished by a suspension—by a refusal to let us see the deed we have expected from the beginning. The impact of their death is thus magnified: "I do adjure the gods to witness how thou hast slain my sons and wilt not suffer me to embrace or bury their dead bodies." It is this closure without closure which adds power and significance to the tragedy. Euripides himself is not oblivious to what he has wrought: "oft do the gods bring things to pass beyond man's expectations; that which we thought would be, is not fulfilled, while for the unlooked-for good finds out a way; and such hath been the issue of this matter."

The third level of suspension is the total omission of the narration of the climatic event at the very end of a play. In *Iphigenia at Aulis* the stalled Achaean fleet awaits the sacrifice of Agamemnon's daughter to provide favorable sailing weather. The plot is built on the inner and interpersonal tensions the impending sacrifice arouses. One version of the play ends with the description of Iphigenia's off-stage sacrifice in the words of a returning messenger (second level suspension). But what most critics agree is the original ending (Feder: 216) omits news of her averted death and translation; the play ends with her being led off to her death. The plot of *Heracleidae* has similar elements. The Argive army under the tyrant Eurystheus is advancing on Athens. To avoid defeat the Athenians must sacrifice a maiden; Hercules' daughter Macaria volunteers. There is much talk of the nobility of her willing sacrifice but after her exit there is no word, not even a report, about the death we know takes place and on which the victory depends. Later, after the arrival of Hercules' son and the rout of the Argives, Eurystheus is led away to a death the audience does not see.

This reticence to portray climactic deaths cannot be explained away by arguments of propriety or the literary taste of critics like Horace. Naturally, some climactic scenes could not be staged; the burning of Troy would have taxed the skills of fifth century dramatists even if they had wanted to enact it. On the other hand, the

tragedians felt free to depict death on stage if and when they chose:
to Sophocles' *Ajax* add the example of Euripides' *Alcestis*. There the
death and "resurrection" of the heroine are acted in plain view. We
must look for another explanation, which lies in the special kind of
response readers have to a scene—in this case, plunging a knife into
a maiden's chest—which is enacted in their imagination rather than
on the stage. The effect, the horror, is not necessarily greater but it
carries its own unique impact. When a tyrant is led away to his
execution at the end of a play, the readers—not the playwright or
other actors—escort the villain, stand him on the appropriate spot,
pronounce his doom, strike the blow, and watch his fall. The event is
established by the structure and foreshadowing of the plot but it is
carried out solely by the readers.

Whatever the precise effect of the endings of the great Athenian
tragedies, the effect was accomplished by clearly recognizable techniques. As we tentatively observed from the plays of Sophocles, the
ancient playwrights tend to have violent murders take place offstage
and typically the report of a messenger is substituted for the action
itself. This is not attributable to queasy stomachs or a sense of social
impropriety; violence and death were at times depicted on the
stage. Most importantly, a sense of openness at the ending of the
plays was achieved by means of a series of predictions regarding the
fates of the characters, by the use of the report of a death in place of
the death, or by the total omission of the climactic scene. These
devices mirror the narrative suspensions at the end of the Homeric
epics and foreshadow the conclusions of other types of Greek literature.

Suspended Endings in Ancient Biography

Some students of narrative question the application of the term
"biography" to any ancient works; others claim it as a legitimate
ancient genre and even include the Gospels in the category.[4] This
study is not the appropriate setting for carrying on the debate over
biography or even for determining the genre of the Gospels. There
is a small group of works which by their attention to the whole life
and development of one person justify the use of the term. Two
contrasting examples are instructive.

[4] Talbert (1977) argues that the gospels should be included in the genre of ancient
biography; Momigliano (1977) provides an analysis of the characteristics of this
important genre.

Xenophon's *Cyropaedia* is an ancient "life" which has been classified as history, historical romance, and biography. Its contents touch on many elements, even rhetoric. Structurally the work betrays a perfect symmetry. It begins with a full description of Cyrus' birth, leads the reader through his exploits and honors, and closes with an account of his death. Two matters complicate the apparent closure. One is the later addition of an eighth book. Some Greek, no doubt less enamoured of Persia than was Xenophon, appended a chronicle of the decline of Cyrus' line. Most scholars assume the *Cyropaedia* ended with Book VII. The other matter is what Xenophon intended and what readers saw in his work. Its idealizing and moralizing tendencies show that the life of Cyrus is in a sense suggestive of the greatness of the Persian Empire and instructive of the noble life. The work's historical action, which is nicely rounded off, is complemented by a didactic element, whose final effect is enacted in the mind of the reader.

In contrast to the high degree of narrative closure in the *Cyropaedia, The Life of Apollonius* by Philostratus is a model of the inconclusive ending. It also shows some self-consciousness about the way a narrative—especially a biography—should end. Philostratus' account of the close of Apollonius' life is filled with uncertainty. He may have been eighty, ninety, or over a hundred when he died. He may have died in Ephesus or in the temple of Athene at Lindus. He may not have died at all but lived on in a temple on Crete. Whether or not he had ever died, Apollonius had become immortal. As proof of his immortality, the biographer assures us that no tomb or cenotaph exists but stories of his divine nature and abilities live on and abound.

What is striking—aside from the uncertainty of the author about the details surrounding Apollonius' death—is the fact that this narrative about the death and immortality of the teacher is an addition to the source-chronicle, the first narrative of the life of Apollonius, on which Philostratus based his treatise. "The memoirs . . . of Apollonius of Tyana which Damis the Assyrian composed" are no longer extant, but Philostratus makes constant reference to them.[5] As for the end of Apollonius' story in Damis' account, there is none. Respecting Appollonius' desire to "slip unobserved from life" (Book

---

[5] Some commentators think that Damis is the literary invention of Philostratus. If, as I assume, the original audience thought of Damis as a genuine source, the literary effect is the same in either case.

XXVIII) Damis told none of the many stories which circulated about the teacher's death. Philostratus' justification for including and concluding with the confusing and contradictory accounts is interesting: "But as for myself I ought not to omit even this, for my story should, I think, have its natural ending." Significantly enough, Philostratus' conclusion is no less certain for all its words than Damis'; and it lacks much of the sense of mystery and reverence which Philostratus sought to achieve. Whatever the relative effects of these two biographies on their original readers would have been, they form an interesting mirror for the New Testament Gospels—Mark, the unfinished biography, and Matthew and Luke, which attempted to append the "natural ending."

Suspended Endings in Ancient Romances

Five Greek romances, or "novels" as they are sometimes called, survive from antiquity. Although they are not well-known to the casual student of classical literature, they enjoyed considerable popularity in their day and steady scholarly attention even now. They are interesting to us not so much for their literary quality as for two other factors. They are popular works; like the Gospels, they lack epic proportions but still tell a good story. And they are "eucatastrophic" works; again like the Gospels, in spite of many ups and downs, a sudden and dramatic reversal for the better results in a happy ending.

In general, the romances achieve full closure. This is due partially to the narrative style. "The straightforward mode of narrative . . .—a beginning *ab ovo*, a linear succession of events, and a definite end" (Hägg: 310) is characteristic. The sense of closure owes itself also to the central theme. "Matrimony, not love, is the fulfillment of the prose romances. It is the goal of respectable marriage that gives breathlessness to the adventures which obstruct consummation and happy release when it is in the end achieved" (Hadas: 11). The beginnings are specific and formulaic in nature: the locus, parentage, nobility, and childhood trauma of the main characters are customarily presented early in the text and in great detail. Foreshadowings of the happy ending are interspersed among the dangers and reversals of the plot. As a rule these novels lack the foreshadowing of major events outside the framework of the narrative. But in several instances a significant degree of openness is nonetheless achieved.

The romance of *Chaereas and Callirhoe* was written by

Chariton in about A.D. 125. Like the others in this genre, the story involves the separation and misadventures of two young lovers. There is no prediction of the outcome in the introduction, but the plot makes it plain that the goal is their reunion. Chariton finally reveals the conclusion as well as his sensitivity to his readers' interest in "how it all turns out" at the beginning of Book VIII.

> Furthermore, I think that this last book will be the most pleasant of all to my readers, and in fact will serve as an antidote to the tragic events of the former ones. No more piracy or slavery or court trials or battles or suicides or war or capture here but true love and lawful marriage. And so I am going to tell you how the goddess brought the truth to light and revealed the unsuspecting loves to each other.

But at the end the reunion leaves much to be desired. The lovers are in a sense together and both are acquitted of the crimes for which they were falsely accused. But after the acquittal there is no token of their "true love" or consummation of their "lawful marriage." Callirhoe goes off to rest. Chaereas recounts his adventures to the men of Syracuse. On her way Callirhoe stops at Aphrodite's temple to pray: "Once again thou hast shown me Chaereas here in Syracuse where as a girl I saw him at thy wish. . . . I beg thee, never again part me from Chaereas but grant us both a happy life, and death together." There is closure here, to be sure; but the private reunion for which the lovers (and the readers) have been longing is not narrated. Callirhoe's closing prayer impels the reader into the near and distant future. So in spite of the sense of closure Chariton has achieved, there remains "the hope or expectation or fear which a character feels at the prospect of the unknown future; in this case its fulfillment falls outside the temporal frame of the romance . . ." (Hägg: 216).

From Xenophon of Ephesus comes *An Ephesian Tale* (about A. D. 200), the story of Habrocomes and Anthia. There are "serious questions about the completeness" of the work (Schmeling: 21) but as it now stands it exhibits full closure. From the start the end is foreshadowed: "It is the custom for young men to find wives here and young girls to select husbands." The expectation for an erotic reunion of the lovers is ever present if restrained. And the end satisfies the expectation with reunion and full recapitulation. That Xenophon was willing to round off his story so completely indicates that the more open endings of some of the other romances were deliberate and voluntary choices of literary technique within the genre.

Like *An Ephesian Tale, An Ethiopian Romance* by Heliodorus (about A. D. 225) fulfills our expectations for the marriage of Theagenes and Chariclea. But in the process the author displays a sophisticated plot structure and time sequence which must not be overlooked. The novel begins *in medias res*. A flashback tells of when the pair had fallen in love; a second flashback relates the birth of Chariclea; and a third brings the story from the end of the first flashback up to where the book begins. The story continues through separation and trial to recognition, reunion, and marriage.

Longus' *Daphnis and Chloe* (about A. D. 250) breaks several molds: it emphasizes a sexual relationship instead of (but not to the exclusion of) marriage, and its ending is more suspended than those of the other romances we have noted. Two lost noble children are rescued and raised together by a shepherd. They fall deeply in love and are sexually stirred. Their innocence and ignorance prevent their passion from leading beyond tender embraces. The pair is separated after a pledge of eternal love. In the midst of harrowing adventures, Daphnis is taught the art of love-making by an older woman. That sexuality and not simply matrimony is meant to be part of the reader's expectation is borne out by the emphasis on this scene and its explicit language. At last the typical rescues, recognition, and reunions occur and the threads of the plot are resolved. But at this point two types of suspension appear. One is the projection into the future of the lives of the lovers: we learn that they live on as shepherds, have two children, and are pious. The second is the omission of the anticipated sexual union. It is alluded to again at the end of the novel but never described as having taken place. Longus was certainly not concerned about offending sensibilities by explicit eroticism; he has already displayed his willingness and talent in that area in the scene with Daphnis and Lycaenion. Rather he has chosen to leave the climax of the romance to the imagination of the reader who has awaited it since the first stirrings of innocent desire and is quite capable of supplying the details.

Like *Daphnis and Chloe*, and again in spite of Hadas' contention that matrimony, not sex, is the chief object in the Greek romances, *The Adventures of Leucippe and Cleitophon* by Achilles Tatius (about A.D. 300) stresses preserved virginity and the sexual union of the main characters. The sexual theme is strong throughout. Cleitophon falls in love with Leucippe but is unsure how to express his affection physically. A cousin gives him instruction in love-making, and he practices by attempting to attract members of the opposite sex. When his first rendezvous with Leucippe is interrupted, he laments, "How long, my dearest, are we to stop at kisses, which are nothing but a prelude?" A second meeting is interrupted by the girl's mother who has been awakened by a dream of a robber with a naked sword. At this point the separation, storms, enslavements, escapes, seductions, and imprisonments carry the adventure to its conclusion. The customary recognitions and reunions take place. But, given the strong emphasis on the erotic side of their relationship, the conclusion is understated and anti-climatic: they arrive at Byzantium, "where we celebrated the marriage for which we so long had prayed." No doubt the reticence is partly due to the shift to respectability common in much ancient romantic literature. Nevertheless, on the basis of this or other conventions, the long unconsummated love of Cleitophon and Leucippe remains unconsummated in the narrative but not in the story which continues to be told by the mind of the reader.

Thus even in this popular form of pure fiction the suspended ending had its place and was used to good effect. This awareness is especially significant in the light of two factors. First, these romances had less tradition to build on. The authors could not rely as much on the ability of their readers to fill in gaps (much less omitted climaxes) automatically from their general store of mythological and historical knowledge. When they failed to narrate a conclusion they were relying heavily on the reader's native ability to convert the structure of the narrative and foreshadowings of the plot into mental closure. The survival of these works is testimony to the success of their ancient readers in this sophisticated process of reading. Second, these stories were based on the fairy-tale motif: separation and trial eventuate in victory, reunion, and a happy ending. The power of the suspended ending is demonstrated by its successful if selective insertion into this, one of the most closed of literary forms.

A pattern of narrative technique has emerged from the endings of ancient as well as modern literary works. There are two broad types of suspended endings—textual and narrative. Textual suspensions are of two varieties. In some literary works critics feel an author intended to write more but left the text incomplete for one reason or another (Aeneid, An Ephesian Tale). In others critics are convinced that the extant ending is a later addition and that the original text ended at an earlier point (Odyssey, Iphigenia at Aulis).

Narrative suspensions are found in those works which conclude with a pervasive sense of openness toward an anticipated future or those which deliberately omit a crucial concluding event. The openness can be created in a variety of ways. Some stories emphasize the on-going life of the main characters by narrating a summary of future events; there is the sense that as life goes on so the story goes on (*Helen, Daphnis and Chloe*). Others conclude with prophecies of the future (*Orestes, Electra*). Still others end with the sense of hope, expectation, or fear (several dramas and romances). The narrative uncertainty at the close of the *Life of Apollonius* complements the emphasis on the subject's immortality.

The second mode of narrative suspension—the omission of a crucial concluding event—is more complex. These omitted events are, of course, anticipated or else their omission would have gone unnoticed. This anticipation is achieved by plot outlines in the opening lines of a work (*Aeneid*); by vague allusion, stated plans, direct prophecy, or themes developed throughout the work (*Iliad*); and by the structural "shape" of the plot (romances, e.g., the expectation of the reunion created the separation and tests of the fairy-tale genre). In most works there is also some literary device at work in the conclusion itself which confirms the reader's expectations and serves as an indicator of the suspended event. Sometimes a final allusion does the job (*Chaereas and Callirhoe*). Especially in Euripides, but also in Homer and elsewhere, a messenger reports the incident which has not been narrated in the natural temporal flow of events (*The Supplicants, Iphigenia at Aulis*). The narrator or a character, even the Chorus, can also function in the role of messenger—announcing what remains undescribed (*The Adventures of Cleitophon and Leucippe*). In these cases the concluding event is incorporated into the text but as discourse not as event. Then again some writers employ a symbol, a metaphor, a synecdoche, for the absent ending. As illustrated by the olive tree bed, the death of Hector, or the death of Turnus, one narrative feature can stand for and suggest a broader, unnarrated conclusion.

These devices have also demonstrated their effect. The temptation to add to open-ended works (Xenophon, Vergil's later "assistants") is but a symptom of the attraction of the suspended ending and the ability of readers to supply mental closure. The raw materials are both intra-narrative (outlines, prophecies, allusions, theme and plot development) and extra-narrative (social customs, cultural norms, and literary traditions). But the power that is generated from the phenomenon is fairly well focused: when readers supply the ending they participate in it and experience it more fully than if the writer had supplied it to them. It remains to be seen if Biblical literature shows any evidence of these phenomena.

CHAPTER IV

"FRAUGHT WITH BACKGROUND": SUSPENDED ENDINGS IN OLD TESTAMENT LITERATURE

> For everything there is a season,
>   and a time for every matter under heaven:
> a time to keep silence,
>   and a time to speak.
>
> (ECCLESIASTES 3.1, 7b)

In whatever sense the Bible might be the Word of God, it is certainly written in a human language. Because it shares at least that characteristic with other human communication, it shares the devices employed by other forms of literary production. Recognizing this basic commonality does not necessarily involve rejecting the many and considerable changes which have occurred in the evolution of literary styles from ancient to modern times. So it is with a sense of caution tinged with confidence that we embark on a study of the functions of silence and suspended endings in the texts of the Bible.

Of the many devices and figures which the language of the Old Testament shares with literature in general, silence and suspension are significant if often overlooked features. Auerbach's seminal essay on "Odysseus' Scar" established the background for the analysis of a certain "economy of style" (Caird: 94) which permeates Hebrew writings. These texts achieve

> the externalisation of only so much of the phenomena as is necessary for the purpose of the narrative, all else left in obscurity; the decisive points of the narrative alone are emphasized, what lies behind is nonexistent; time and place are unidentified and call for interpretation; thoughts and feelings remain unexpressed, are only suggested by the silence and fragmentary speeches; the whole permeated

> with the most unrelieved suspense and directed toward a single goal . . . remains mysterious and "fraught with background" (Auerbach: 11).

Auerbach's observations are instructive: what is non-existent in the text must and can be supplied by interpretation, and silence or the fragments of communication which are present suggest what is not present.

To Auerbach's insights must be added other general observations; Robert Alter supplies the supporting theory and Herman Gunkel an appropriate illustration. First, about what matters are Old Testament texts likely to be silent? Motives, emotions, physical characteristics, clothing, tools, and other accoutrements of daily life—in short, characterization—are frequently undescribed (Alter: 114). In the story of the destruction of Sodom and Gomorrah Abraham journeys to a spot where he can look down on the fiery ruins, containing (he assumes) the ashes of his nephew Lot. The narrative tells us only that he "beheld, and lo, the smoke of the land went up like the smoke of a furnace" (Genesis 19:28). "For the story-teller this little scene is plainly not of interest because of the thing that happened but because of the thoughts which Abraham must have thought, and yet he does not tell us what these thoughts were" (Gunkel: 60). Second, how do we sense these undescribed features and get at such things as character and motive? At times we cannot; but by a "set of . . . supple techniques" Old Testament texts provide "fragmentary data" which provide an inferential base (Alter: 115, 126). One specific technique is to record in dialogue what is unrecorded in the narrative;[1] its obverse is the account of some action which presupposes an emotion, an attitude, or even a whole conversation. The latter is the case with the story at hand; the narrator "merely reports to us the outward incidents, and we are obliged to supply the really important point ourselves" (Gunkel: 60). And third, why this reticence, why these silences? Whether the motive is literary (the form being employed) or theological (the view being embraced), whether the means are conscious or unconscious, the silences seem purposeful (Alter: 114–115). And among those purposes may be the very result Gunkel described in the reading of this

[1] Alter: 182; "As a rule, when a narrative event in the Bible seems important, the writer will render it mainly through dialogue, so the transitions from narrative to dialogue provide in themselves some implicit measure of what is deemed essential."

little scene—the obligation of the readers to think Abraham's thoughts for him.

Form criticism has attributed the lack of personal and circumstantial detail to the "attritional effect of oral transmission" (Caird: 9 5), a slow but steady pruning of all but the skeleton. These omissions were usually natural, as the material was handed down story by story. In spite of Caird's objections, we must accept with gratitude the critical discovery that many omissions are in fact due to the process of transmission. The Homeric epics are the result of an even longer and more complex process of oral transmission, to be sure; but their fixed poetic form made them less vulnerable to such attrition than the more loosely organized Biblical texts. Still the form-critical explanation does not account for every instance; the fact is that there is more than personal and circumstantial detail omitted from some Old Testament texts. At the same time, although Auerbach has done great service in pointing out the obscurity of the background details in Biblical texts, he has not dealt with those texts in which the "decisive points of the narrative" are not only not emphasized but are themselves non-existent. It is to these texts, especially those whose conclusions are in some way omitted, that we turn our attention.

On the basis of examples of open and omitted endings in Greek literature we can establish a series of working categories by which we may delineate the various types of omissions. There are two kinds of conclusions which have attracted our attention—open-ended conclusions (A) and omitted conclusions (B). Three procedures are characteristically used to achieve a sense of open-endedness. Some narratives end with a summary of concluding events, a succinct narrative statement of facts which draw past plots together and imply a future sense of on-going life (A1). Other narratives end with a prophecy of future events whose eventual fulfillment is assured (A2). Yet another group ends simply on a note of hope and expectation (A3). Narratives whose conclusions are actually omitted imply the absent ending either by means of content (B1) or form (B2). At times plot outlines at the very beginning of a work supply the information necessary for reading the omitted ending (B1a). Allusions, prophecies, or foreshadowing throughout the text may accomplish the same purpose (B1b). Or a final element, a closing allusion or the report of an incident in discourse rather than the description of the event in narrative, may stand for the omitted conclusions (B1c). Often the balanced structure of a work or the repeated structures within it provide the clue to the content of the omitted ending (B2). The story summaries which follow fall roughly into these same categories and demonstrate the use of many of the same techniques of suspension observed in Greek and Roman literature.

Shorter Narratives

The story of Jephthah supplies a simple example of a totally omitted ending which is implied by a final indirect reference (B1c). In Judges 11:29–40 we read of a father who vows to sacrifice the first thing he sees upon returning home, if only YHWH gives him the victory in battle. The battle won, Jephthah returns to find his only daughter coming to meet him, dancing and making music to celebrate his homecoming. The grief-stricken father rehearses his vow; the girl accepts her fate and asks only for some time to mourn her virginity. The detailed account of the rash father and the noble daughter ends with an amazing stillness. "At the end of the two months, she returned to her father, who did with her according to his vow which he had made." The reticence in describing the act of sacrifice was certainly not to spare the readers from the sight of blood or the fact of death; the book of Judges is perhaps the bloodiest in the Bible. Theological horror at the thought of the pagan practice of child sacrifice may enter the picture. But from a literary point of view, the act, its poignancy, and the aversion the father feels toward the deed he must do are all enhanced in the reader's mind by the understated, almost unstated description of the death.

Marriage Stories. But most Old Testament stories employ a very sparse conclusion which leaves the reader with a sense of openness. One type of story which characteristically uses a muted conclusion is the marriage story. Three examples set the pattern and suggest some possible explanations. In each case the stories fall into the category of conclusions told by succinct summary (A1). In Genesis 24, Abraham gives his servant elaborate instructions for procuring a wife for Isaac from Mesopotamia. The journey of the servant, his prayer for providential guidance, and Rebekah's kind deeds and kind words are all recited in detail. We learn of Laban's elaborate oriental hospitality; the servant recites Abraham's message and recounts the meeting with Rebekah. An agreement is made, gifts are exchanged, and they return to Canaan. After this long, detailed narration, the story rushes to a close; the end is narrated but in a clipped, anti-climactic style. "Then Isaac brought her into the tent, and took Rebekah, and she became his wife; and he loved her."

The story of Jacob's marriage (Genesis 29:1–30) follows the same pattern of journey and encounter. Jacob falls in love with Rachel in the midst of a complex story of bargaining and betrayal; reversal occurs when Rachel's older sister is substituted at the ceremony and Jacob must labor seven more years for the right to marry Rachel. After all the intrigue, after all the anticipation of the eventual union of the two lovers separated by geography, culture, religion, and (worst of all) plotting parents, the end is muted, without detail, matter-of-fact: "Laban gave his daughter Rachel to wife. So Jacob went in to Rachel also, and he loved Rachel more than Leah, and served Laban for another seven years."

Like Jacob, Moses (Exodus 2:15–21) travelled to a foreign land, arrived at a well, and gave timely aid to his future wife. The detailed narration of Moses' arrival, his fight with the shepherds, his aid to Jethro's daughters, and Jethro's hospitality are not balanced by the description of the outcome of the series of events. "And Moses was content to dwell with the man, and he gave Moses his daughter Zipporah."

These stories have stated conclusions, but their muted nature makes them instructive for analyzing stories which seem to lack any satisfactory conclusion. Why are these endings so brief, so devoid of the passion and intensity of the stories themselves? One answer is that the endings are foregone conclusions; we have read the ending so consistently in the beginning and the middle that it demands only the briefest mention at the end. Another answer is that the theological emphasis dominates the narrative structure: the fact that God was working it all out all along assured that it would work out and in a sense is more important to the writer (and the original reader) than how it worked out. In other words, the matter-of-fact ending forces us back into the story and re-emphasizes the providential aspect which necessitated such an outcome; we read the beginning and the middle in the ending.

Miracle Stories. In general, Old Testament miracle stories omit some key element which modern readers would find significant— the details of the miracle, the results of the miracle, or the description of the miracle itself. "The miracle story is not to be confused with the miracle event: these stories never narrate the miracle itself because the miracle is by nature divine mystery" (Betz: 69). The event may be omitted out of reverence, but there are other literary and theological reasons for the omission of the conclusions of these stories. Culley (1976:69f, 93–94) has demonstrated a structural pattern in Old Testament miracle stories which illuminates how these stories end. A Problem is brought to someone's attention. That person's Response is usually in the form of an instruction regarding an Object and an Action. Finally the miraculous Result is reported. Culley (1976:93–94) also points out that the result is less detailed than the rest of the narrative: "Normally, the narrative simply states briefly what has occurred." Exodus 15:22–25a clearly illustrates his point. Having set the scene, the author reports a Problem (they could not drink the water because it was bitter). Moses passes the complaint on to the Lord (What shall we drink?). The divine Response instructs Moses to take a tree (Object) and throw (Action) it into the water. The water becomes sweet (Result). But notice how silent the ending is compared to the clamoring of the story: no joyful shouts balance the complaints; no words of thanks replace the questions and criticism. We are not even told that the people drank any of the sweetened water or stopped their murmuring. Much of this we assume, but we are told nothing directly.

The suspension in the ending of other miracle stories is more marked, so much so that we should amend Culley's statement to say that sometimes the narrative simply does not state what has occurred. Exodus 17:1–6 tells another story about the lack of water (Problem). The complaints and criticisms are more graphically and repeatedly described than in Exocus 15: we learn that the people are about to stone Moses. But when Moses asks for help, God tells him (Response) to take his rod (Object) and strike (Action) a rock, "and water may come out of it, that the people may drink" (foreshadowed Result). The account quickly closes with these words: "And Moses did so, in the sight of the elders of Israel." Did water come forth? Did the people drink? Did they stop their murmuring? We answer yes, but why?

First, on the basis of suggestions in the story, the foreshadowed result expressed in the dialogue between God and Moses, we assume that what God predicted will occur. Second, on the basis of the abbreviated ending that is there, we read much that is not: the little word "so" (ken) carries the full weight of the unnarrated action, and if the action then the miracle, and if the miracle then the solution to the problem. And third, the structural pattern of the miracle stories leads us to expect the result which occurs in such stories—the problem is solved, the prophecy fulfilled, the result reached.[2]

A final example comes from II Kings 4:1–7. A prophet has died leaving a widow and two children about to be claimed as slaves by the man's creditors (Problem). Elisha instructs (Response) her to take her only possession, a jar of oil (Object), to borrow vessels from her neighbors, and to pour the oil into the vessels (Action). She does and miraculously the contents of the little jar fill all the vessels (Result). Then Elisha instructs (Response 2) her to take the oil (Object 2) and "sell the oil and pay your debts" (Action 2), "and you and your sons can live on the rest" (Result 2). Thus the story closes with no word of the actual performance of the action or of the results of the action. Did she go? Did she sell? Did they live on in peace? The result remains foreshadowed in the command of the prophet. But the closing command to act and the promise of result not only suggests the suspended ending but stands for it in the text. And the structural pattern—not only the general pattern of miracle stories but in this case the fact that the woman obeyed the first instructions to good effect—gives us grounds for reading the ending that is not there.

Longer Narratives

As with the shorter forms, book-length narratives in the Old Testament display a whole spectrum of styles of conclusion, from full closure to open-endedness to omitted endings. Even though they form a five-volume narrative with a unity of its own, the books of the Pentateuch have been and are read as semi-independent units. Exodus has an expansive ending which looks forward to an indeterminate future of journeying under God's guidance (Category A2, 3). "Throughout all their journeys" recurs like a refrain in the closing verses, turning the attention of the reader to the unnarrated events which lie ahead of the wanderers. The book of Numbers creates tremendous anticipation for the re-entry of the Israelites into Canaan (Category A2, 3). The journey which fills its pages is ostensibly the journey to Canaan. Along the way instruction for life and worship in Canaan prepares the people for their ever-present goal. Twelve men reconnoiter Canaan, an army tries to force entry into

---

[2] This omission is no accident; a similar story in Numbers 20 describes the striking of the rock, the abundant flow of water, and the slaking of the thirst of people and cattle.

Canaan, and another circuitous journey brings the nation to the borders of Canaan. The whole book anticipates an end which never comes; the last words of the book leave the expectation tantalizingly unfulfilled, the people camped opposite Jericho, the goal which they have not reached. In Deuteronomy the suspense is increased by the suspension of the narrative of the long-awaited return and the substitution of a series of historical and hortatory speeches by Moses (Category B1b,c). The goal is assured but only because it is assumed; the reader lives with the reality of its fulfillment although the narrative leaves us staring across the Jordan at the Promised Land.[3]

In many respects the book of Ruth is the most artistically wrought narration in the Old Testament: the personal tragedy of Naomi is resolved, the love of Ruth and Boaz is consummated, and the historical note with which the book begins ("when the judges governed") is balanced by the mention of David in the closing genealogy. But it is this last element, the genealogy, which causes the narrative of Ruth to stretch far into the future, to David her royal descendant, to the kingdom of the Davidic line, and to the Messianic expectation of Jews and Christians alike (Category A1, 3).

The conclusion of II Kings is not merely open-ended; the happy ending the reader longs for is omitted but alluded to by a final feature (B1c). This long chronicle of Israelite history ends not with the statement of the fact that the exiled Jews eventually returned from Babylon or even the clear promise that they would return, much less the actual description of the return. It ends with an odd anecdote about the exiled king of Judah.

> Evil-merodach king of Babylon . . . graciously freed Jehoiachin king of Judah from prison; and he spoke kindly to him and gave him a seat above the seats of the kings who were with him in Babylon. So Jehoiachin put off his prison garments. And every day of his life he dined regularly at the king's table; and for his allowance, a regular allowance was given him by the king, every day a portion, as long as he lived.

The anecdotal conclusion is a clear synecdoche for the full-scale restoration of the fortunes of the nation. In the midst of exile lives

---

[3] Deuteronomy 34:66: "but no man knows the place of his burial to this day." Like Oedipus in *Oedipus at Colonnus* and Jesus in the Gospel of Mark, there is no body; this exclusion has its own minor but significant part to play in a story whose power is at least partially generated by what is excluded from the text.

hope; in the midst of disgrace lives honor; in the life of the Davidic dynasty lives the people.

Among the poetic books of the Old Testament, the Song of Songs is the most open-ended, its loose plot relatively unfulfilled but full of expectation (A3). The series of lyric poems weave the story of a rustic maiden and her royal suitor. The longing for each other, the sensuous descriptions of each other's beauty, and the eager preparations for the imminent wedding all create the expectation of a union. But the book ends on that note of unrelieved expectation. The bridegroom calls, "my companions are listening for your voice; let me hear it." The bride echoes the sentiment in her final words: "Make haste, my beloved, and be like a gazelle or a young stag upon the mountains of spices." Only the pattern of separation and reunion and the anticipation of the closing pleas suggest the fulfillment, but they are sufficient.

II Chronicles ends with a command to act rather than the action itself. Cyrus king of Persia establishes an edict that the exiled Jews are to return from Babylon and rebuild their temple; as if to each Jew, Cyrus issues the command, "Let him go up." This final exhortation is not only the end of the two-volume Chronicles; it is also the note on which the Hebrew Bible ends, since in the Hebrew canon II Chronicles stands last. Thus the whole Old Testament ends, as it were, on a command which creates a sense of hope—not only for the fulfillment of this specific promise but for the fulfillment of all the promises of YHWH in every age (an interesting combination of Categories A1, A3, and B1c).

Of course not all Old Testament texts have open or suspended endings. Joshua achieves full literary closure on the biographical and national levels. Esther also demonstrates remarkable literary unity. But these examples of open-ended and unfulfilled plots remind us not only of the common use of the narrative device but also of the ways in which the device was effected. We turn now to two texts—Genesis from the Torah and Jonah from the Prophets—for a more detailed look at the function of silence and suspension in the Old Testament. Each of those texts employs openness and omission (A and B) and the various techniques for achieving them which we have observed.

Genesis is a beginning both doctrinally and literarily. It relates the beginnings of creative activity, of human life, of religions and social institutions, and of a chosen people. But it is also the first chapter of the five-volume Torah, of the multi-volume book we call

the Old Testament, and of the Bible, a whole library in a book. And
yet Genesis is a literary entity. It displays a strong degree of unity
and closure. The Hebrews are at last honored and secure; the last of
the partiarchs dies, having led his people to peace and prosperity;
the sons of Jacob are reconciled to their rejected brother; and the
story of Joseph comes to a convincing end.

In spite of the rounding off which operates on several levels, a
sense of openness remains. The Israelites are still in Egypt, still in
exile, not in their homeland, the land of promise. "The book . . .
ends on a muted note".[4] But the muted note is not one that is likely
to die out; it holds the reader in anticipation of the outburst of a full
symphonic climax. For the ending turns our thoughts to another
land, and to a future time. The last words in the text are "in Egypt,"
but all eyes are turned on Canaan. The journey has come to an end
which is not an end: "The stay in Egypt is but a passing phase, a
sojourn; the focal point continues to be the Promised Land"
(Speiser: 377).

Of crucial interest to this study is not so much why the writer
chose to close the book of Genesis in such a way as how he prepared
his readers to read "Canaan" into a narrative which ends "in Egypt."
Suggestion and foreshadowings of a permanent habitation in Canaan
are the most obvious means. Beginning with the call of Abraham in
Genesis 12, the goal of the plans and actions of the patriarchs has
been Canaan and all it symbolized—a special land for a special
people. Divine promise forms the surest kind of foreshadowing; it
must inevitably be fulfilled. So it is that when the author of Genesis
has God say of Canaan, "To your descendants I will give this land,"
we have the assurance that they will reach their goal. This early
foreshadowing is re-enforced near the end of the narrative by the
solemn declaration of the dying patriarch Joseph: "I am about to die;
but God will visit you, and bring you up out of this land to the land
which he swore to Abraham, to Isaac, and to Jacob" (Genesis 50:24).
On a more personal level Joseph foretells a return which Genesis
does not record: "God will visit you, and you shall carry my bones
from here" (Genesis 50:25). The book which ends in Egypt foreshadows geographical removal from Egypt to Canaan, national establishment of the people in Canaan, and personal burial of Joseph

---

[4] Simpson: 829; compare the comment of Dorothy Sayers (1963:29) on the endings
of the *Iliad* and the *Song of Roland*.

in the land of his forebears. These events are never described but never in doubt.

A second approach to reading the ending of Genesis is to map the structures within the book and compare them to the narrative with which the book closes.

	ABRAHAM (Gen. 12)	ISAAC (Ch. 26)	JACOB (28–33)	JACOB (Ch. 50)	JOSEPH (Ch. 50)
RESIDENCE	Canaan	Canaan	Canaan	Canaan	Canaan
CRISIS	Famine	Famine	Rivalry	Famine	Rivalry
SOJOURN	Egypt	Philistia	Paddan-aram	Egypt	Egypt
RETURN	Canaan	Canaan	Canaan	Canaan (corpse)	[x]

The early part of the Abraham narrative (chapters 12–13) supplies an interesting paradigm. Abraham settles in the land of Canaan but a famine drives him to Egypt. After some misadventures there, he is escorted by Pharaoh's men out of the country and Abraham returns to Canaan. The pattern is duplicated in the lives of Abraham's son and grandson.[5] Isaac left Canaan because of a famine, had some misadventures of his own in Philistia (he was specifically instructed not to go to Egypt), and eventually left there to follow his flocks around southern Canaan (Genesis 26). As a result of sibling rivalry, Jacob fled his homeland in another direction. He spent years in Paddan-aram earning a wife and a fortune; but as soon as the opportunity came he returned to Canaan, impelled by a divine mandate but in the face of his brother's wrath (Genesis 28–33). Joseph's is the specific journey whose ending is suspended at the close of Genesis; but he did undertake a journey in behalf of his father Jacob which parallels his own foreshadowed but unfinished journey from Canaan to Egypt to Canaan. Jacob died, was embalmed, and mourned in Egypt, but not before Joseph had sworn to bury him in Canaan. "I am about to die: in my tomb which I hewed out for myself in the land of Canaan, there shall you bury me" (Genesis 50:5). So Joseph led a grand funeral procession back to Canaan where Jacob was buried beside Abraham and Isaac. Thus Joseph had already escorted his father's body on the same journey on which we know his body would later be taken. Joseph's story follows

[5] The story of Isaac's near sacrifice on Mount Moriah takes the young man from home to exile and near-death to providential rescue and back home (Genesis 22).

the same pattern. Only the final function—a function which the paradigm presupposes—is omitted, left to the informed imagination of the reader.

Thirdly, there are several features in the ending of Genesis which provide material for reading the unnarrated endings. The physical remains of Joseph hold our attention at the end of the opus. His remains are embalmed, not likely to decompose in Egypt, truly remaining, ready for the return we anticipate. And he is in a coffin, not a grave but a coffin, not a final resting place but a means of conveyance. The body and the coffin and the words which prophesy his burial in Canaan are synecdoches for the people and the journey and their settlement in the land of promise. "The coffin . . . became a standing exhortation to Israel to turn its eyes away from Egypt to Canaan . . . and to wait in the patience of faith for the fulfillment of the promise" (Keil and Delitzsch: 413). It stands for the readers as a sign of the fulfillment of a literary promise which we in good faith read into the silence of the text's conclusion.

The prophetic story of Jonah is not as familiar as the "fish story" it contains. A popular Israelite prophet is commanded to preach an unpopular message of divine destruction in Nineveh, the chief city of the cruel Assyrians. He flees on a ship headed for Tarshish (Spain?). A vicious wind abates only when the sailors toss Jonah— the one whose disobedience to his god has caused the storm—into the sea. He prays for deliverance from inside the fish God sent to bear him to dry land. A second commission is heeded: Jonah goes to Nineveh and proclaims that God will destroy the city unless they repent. The Ninevites repent, but Jonah has gone outside the city to watch the destruction. A plant sprouts and shades Jonah until a worm devours it. The story ends with God chiding Jonah for caring more for the fate of a plant than for the Ninevites.

But what happened to Jonah? Did he remain? Did he return to Israel? Did he repent of his evil wishes? Did he become as compassionate as the God he represented? Some might say that these are the wrong questions, that the book is not "about" Jonah but the righteousness of God and the repentance of the Ninevites. Still the book is heavily biographical and readers come to the end with unanswered questions. Knox calls it "the most striking exception" to the norm of full closure which he finds in the Hebrew scriptures. Jewish interpreters have often viewed Jonah as an unfinished work; rabbinic tradition relates more experiences in the fish's belly, reports that he attained old age, and informs us of his immortality (Harrison:

905). But the theory that the book is unfinished, the attempts to close out his life story, and the admission that the ending is at the least abrupt, are all views which fall short of an appreciation for the dynamic of the suspended ending. "The sharpest blow is struck; the deepest point of contradiction in Jonah's attitude is exposed and with that the parable breaks off. When the knife has been driven in to the hilt, what more remains to be done? It is unnecessary for the prophetic writer to add any explanation" (Smart: 873).

Again, three factors make full literary closure unnecessary. First, foreshadowing in the story suggests the deliverance of Jonah from his bigotry and recalcitrance: the sailors were rescued from the storm, Jonah from the fish, Jonah again from his foolish flight, and the Ninevites from their evil ways. The theme which resounds through the whole book came through the testimony of Jonah himself: "Deliverance belongs to the Lord." Second, the ending itself contains a common device, the substitution of dialogue for action. God speaks to Jonah of the prophet's pity for the withered plant and reminds him of the divine compassion for the Ninevites. The unstated assumption is that Jonah should at least pity these people. This lesson, God's final words to the prophet, is the discourse which replaces the narration of Jonah's repentance; "for a prophetic book the words of God are normally a sufficient ending" (Knox: 22).

Third, the structure of the book not only provisionally answers the unanswered questions but highlights those questions by placing the answers in the mind of the reader rather than in the text.

	I (Jonah 1–2)		II (Jonah 3–4)
Al	*Narrative setting*	Al	*Narrative setting*
	The word of the Lord came to Jonah Arise, go to Nineveh But Jonah rose to flee to Tarshish		The word of the Lord came to Jonah the second time Arise, go to Nineveh So Jonah arose and went to Nineveh
A2	*Mythic setting*	A2	*Mythic setting*
	Journey west/sea/wind		Journey east/land/wind
A3	*Narrative action*	A3	*Narrative action*
	Sailors as self-deliverers action (cast out wares) prayer (to God)		*Ninevities as self-deliverers* message (God will destroy city)

rationale*
message (God caused storm)
worship (feared the Lord)

faith (believed God)
action (fast in sackcloth)
prayer (to God)
rationale*

(*"Perhaps the god will give a thought to us, that we do not perish.")

(*"Who knows, God may yet repent and turn from his fierce anger, so that we perish not.")

God as deliverer of sailors
calmed sea

God as deliverer of Ninevities
repented of destruction

B1 *Narrative setting*

Jonah in belly of fish

B1 *Narrative setting*

Jonah in booth

B2 *Mythic setting*

fish/weeds

B2 *Mythic setting*

plant/worm

B3 *Narrative action*

Jonah as self-deliverer

only of self
in sea—rescue

B3 *Narrative action*

Jonah as self-deliverer

only of self
on land—death

God as deliverer of Jonah

"But I with the voice of thanksgiving will sacrifice to thee; what I have vowed I will pay. Deliverance belongs to the Lord."

[God as deliverer of Jonah]?

[x]

[Will he give thanks, sacrifice?]
[Will he keep his vows?]
[Will he recognize God as deliverer of himself and all people?]

The two structural sections of the book of Jonah parallel each other perfectly except for the final section, the suspended ending, where the reader's questions replace narrative action. The literary suspension raises those questions forcibly in the mind of the reader and the structural pattern provides a framework for answering them, at least tentatively, in the affirmative.

These explorations of the suspended endings in Old Testament texts have offered a testing ground for the application of theories about the process of suspension, its purpose, and the preparation of the reader to read it intelligently. Suggestive foreshadowing, structural patterning, and the synecdochal function of the ending have emerged as key interpretive factors. It remains to compare the texts of the New Testament and test them against these emerging principles before they can be applied to the Gospel of Mark and the interpretation of its conclusion.

Chapter V

"THINGS UNSEEN": SUSPENSED ENDINGS IN NEW TESTAMENT LITERATURE

> Now hope that is seen is not hope. For who hopes for
> what he sees? But if we hope for what we do not see,
> through patience we have eager expectation.
>
> --PAUL (Romans 8:24–25)

As a collection of written documents, the New Testament shares with all literature certain customary traits. These traits surface in texts like Mark as well as those like Luke or Hebrews which approach a more literary style. Thus we expect the phenomena we have observed in other literature, ancient as well as modern, to characterize New Testament texts. In fact, even though hiddenness is a characteristic of all language, reticence of all expression, and silence of all speech—even though texts of all types and times exhibit lacunae, suppression, exclusion, and suspension—these qualities are not only present but are especially appropriate to New Testament writings. Content can be molded by form, but in the case of the Gospels at least "[t]he new speech and speech-forms of the Gospel followed the law of Gospel and of Christ himself: humiliation and incognito" (Wilder: 37). In the Gospels themselves there is a great paucity of personal detail and background information. This tendency carries over into the letters, Christian texts which adopted the fairly fixed Hellenistic epistolary form. Even the book of Acts which seems to aim most directly at the goal of historicity demonstrates a dearth of circumstantial detail and wants for complete closure.

Form critics have demonstrated that the process of oral transmission accounts for many of these gaps. But some of the significant silences cannot be explained on that basis. It is the literariness, the very textuality of the expression, which produces some silences.

> Once a text is formed, the original character of the gospel
> was transformed. The elements of silence and embodiment
> become far more subtle. The experience of silence in the
> presence of the embodied is now transmitted by the rhythm
> of the language and by the experience of the incommen-
> surability between the text and the sacred acts to which
> they witness (Davis: 93).

Thus we look to the texts themselves and to the literary devices,
sophisticated or simple, with which they were woven for an understanding of the suspended elements and the senses they communicate.

Suspended Elements in the New Testament

Our main interest is in New Testament stories whose endings
are omitted; these stories form the background for an informed
reading of the ending of Mark. But we begin with a series of
examples of internal omissions to demonstrate the facility with
which New Testament writers could imply and New Testament
readers could understand material unstated in the texts. This tendency and this ability are crucial for our eventual interpretation of
Mark's conclusion.

Suspensions often take the form of minor matters of background, isolated facts, or incidental details which would flesh out
our knowledge but are left tantalizing unstated. Allusions to events
otherwise unnarrated are not uncommon. Luke 13:1 refers to some
"Galileans whose blood Pilate had mingled with their sacrifices."
Nothing is known of this event; it is not related in the Gospels or by
Josephus. When, where, and why it happened are not known. It is
unlikely that even Luke's first century audience would have heard of
the incident itself. John 7:42 records a debate late in Jesus' ministry
over his identity; one group questions, "Is the Christ to come from
Galilee? Has not the scripture said that the Christ is descended from
David and comes from Bethlehem. . . .?" What is striking is that
John does not even mention the birth of Jesus much less the place of
this birth. This allusion certainly appeals to the general knowledge
of the late first-century Christian community; but the allusion to an
omitted fact has other potential effects, notably the need of the
reader to add the prophetic background to the statement and tacitly
identify Jesus as Messiah. The two examples demonstrate that gospel writers could allude to totally unknown as well as extremely
well-known events, in each case with good literary effect.

Gospel writers also exclude information which they themselves lead us to expect. Matthew 10 records elaborate instructions for an evangelistic journey which is not narrated. Whether or not the author intends for his reader to think that the journey took place immediately, took place later in Jesus' ministry, or could only occur after the resurrection and commission (Matthew 28:18–20), the expectation and visualization of a missionary tour has been created in the mind of the reader apart from any narration of it (Johnson: 376). Marin (1976:154) is correct to point out (even though he may make too much of the paradigmatic effect of) Mark's failure to describe the payment of the silver to Judas. Matthew reports that Judas was paid at the time of his offer to betray Jesus, but Mark's account only refers to the promise of payment. Judas agreed to deliver Jesus. But what of the payment? Matthew creates his own muted sense of absence by telling how Judas rejected the blood money. But Mark's omission is more radical and more suggestive.

These last examples comprise but one version of unfulfilled foreshadowing. Luke employs the device in 4:13: Satan suspends the temptation of Jesus "until an opportune time." The readers are never told when that time arrives. Are we to connect it with 22:3 ("Then Satan entered Judas") or 22:31 ("Simon, Simon, behold Satan demanded to have you")? Or are we to read for ourselves a renewal of temptation into the mocking words spoken to Jesus as he hung on the cross: "If you are the King of the Jews, save yourself!" (Luke 23:37)? The open, unfulfilled suggestion sharpens the readers' awareness of the possibilities for testing throughout the gospel. John 3:4 mentions that "John [the Baptist] had not yet been put into prison." But in all the later references to the forerunner in this Gospel (3:26, 27; 4:1; 5:33, 36; 10:40, 41), there is no description of his imprisonment or further reference to it. The reader is left to fill in the event on the basis of tradition (compare Mark's detailed account in 6:14–29) or imagination. But whether or not any given reader is able to reconstruct the details of an unnarrated incarceration, the ominous note of opposition has been struck and will sound like a dissonant undertone throughout the rest of the account.[1]

One longer and more significant omission within a New Testament text deserves our attention. The Last Supper of Jesus with his disciples forms a climactic moment in each of the Synoptic Gospels. The ministry of Jesus and his relationship with the disciples are at a

---

[1] Another minor example of lack of fulfillment is found in John 1:51.

turning point; he is poised between life and death, presence and absence, brotherhood and betrayal. The event was so important that the narration of the event itself had taken form in the tradition of the early church and is presented by Paul *as a narrative* in the midst of a letter (I Corinthians 11:23ff.). Such treatment is not even accorded the event of the crucifixion which in Paul remains a fact and tenet of faith but not a narrative. But this climactic event is told in the Synoptic and Pauline accounts with a striking terseness (Simon: 74). All facets of the meal are omitted; muted voices and a few suggestive acts are all we know about what was probably an elaborate meal celebrating the Passover and a complex conversation anticipating Jesus' death. The expectations built up by the detailed preparations for the meal—including the complicated procurement of the room— are not fulfilled by the sparse narrative itself.

But John's Gospel is completely silent on this climactic event which initiated the central Christian rite of worship. The evangelist who relates the most (chapters 13–16) about the events and conversations in the upper room that night also omits the most. After 13:2 no temporal or spatial markers orient the reader, until 18:1. There is no mention of the meal itself, the purpose for their assembly. And the institution of the memorial meal is omitted.

The author has, however, given the readers provision for reading the climactic event which was not written—provision for reading it in his gospel and in its proper place. John 6 provides syntactical and thematic clues for the mental reconstruction of the narrative. John's account of the feeding of the five thousand employs language reminiscent of the traditional Synoptic accounts of the Lord's Supper.

Luke 22:17–20	*I Cor. 11:23–25*	*John 6:11*
He took bread	Jesus took bread	Jesus then took the loaves,
and when he had given thanks	and when he had given thanks	and when he had given thanks
he broke it and gave it to them. . . .	he broke it. . . .	he distributed them. . . ;
And he took a cup. . . .	In the same way also the cup. . . .	so also the fish. . . .

The rhetorical parallels are obvious but the thematic preparation is just as clear. The feeding miracle is followed by a discourse on Jesus as the bread of life, the meaning of the miracle after all.

Appended are the cryptic words, "he who eats my flesh and drinks my blood has eternal life"—echoes of the eucharistic dicta, "Take, eat; this is my body," and "Drink of it, all of you; for this is my blood of the covenant." Whether or not the account in John 6 is John's eucharistic narrative, it places traditional eucharistic language and themes in the minds of the audience and prepares them to fill in the gap in John 13–17.[2]

Another Johannine feature supplies a basis for sensing the narrative of the Last Supper which is not there. The unique description of Jesus washing the feet of the disciples (John 13:1–11) is, like the feeding of the five thousand, syntactically and thematically suggestive of the Lord's Supper. The characters (Jesus and the disciples) and the setting (during supper) are the same. There are also a number of corresponding narrative elements: the cup and the basin, the distribution of the bread and cup and the movement of Jesus from one to the other, the action of pouring, and the emphasis on repetition of the eating and washing. Thus embedded in the footwashing are the echoes of the omitted ritual meal.[3]

Why is the narrative of the institution of the Lord's Supper excluded? An accidental omission is unlikely. However suggestive of the upper room event, the feeding miracle in John 6 is surely more than a misplaced account of the final meal and thus insufficient to explain the total exclusion of that meal. Some commentators infer "that the evangelist deliberately omitted the institution to correct an extravagant sacramentalism" (Howard: 678), that is, to avoid the danger of having the meaning of the event "overlaid by materialistic beliefs" (Morris: 610). For whatever reason, the event is unnarrated but foreshadowed and anticipated by theme, by structure, and by tradition to such an extent that we sense the presence of the event when we arrive at the appropriate place in John's narrative. The result is an emphasis on the "inner significance" of the meal, its atemporal features (reaching into the past and into the future as well

---

[2] For further comments on this connection, see Brown (1966); Simon (1975:74); Morris (1971); and Howard (1952:678).

[3] Even John's description of Jesus's prediction of Judas' betrayal is suggestive of the eucharistic account:

Luke 22:19	*John 13:26–27*
And he took bread	So when he had dipped the morsel
and gave it to them	he gave it to Judas. . . .
saying, . . .	Jesus said to him, . . .
Do this. . . .	do quickly. . . .

as fixed in the present of the text), and its symbolic value (Morris: 610; Howard: 678–679). These aspects are present in the Synoptic and Pauline accounts; but it is the suspended but sensed account of John's Gospel which draws our attention to them.

Suspended Endings in Shorter Narratives

Rhetorical and narrative silences and suppressions appear throughout the New Testament literature; but it is the suspended endings of shorter and longer narrative units which provide proof of the possibility of a suspended ending in Mark and practice for reading intelligently the ending which is not there. Miracle stories, encounter stories, pronouncement stories, and parables are examples of smaller formal units whose narratives may or may not achieve closure in the text itself. The gospels of Matthew and John and the book of Acts form a group of lengthier texts whose endings can be compared with Mark's.

The categories of types and methods of final suspension developed in our study of Greco-Roman literature (Chapter III) and applied in the analysis of Old Testament literature (Chapter IV) will be used again for the classification of these examples from the New Testament. (As before, however, our main purpose is not cataloguing or classification, but the recognition of suspension, of the methods used to provide closure in spite of the suspension, and of the effect of that suspension on the readers of the text.) Open-ended conclusions (A) are those whose endings provide a sense of on-going life (A1), or the prophecy of further fulfillment (A2), or simply a note of hopeful expectation (A3). Those stories or books whose conclusions are seemingly absent (B) may supply plot outlines (B1a), foreshadowing (B1b), or a closing allusion (B1c), each of which may offer the reader with the information for sensing the absent ending. Other omitted endings may be implied and intuited from the structure of the work (B2).

Miracle stories. The tendency not to narrate the core of a miracle story, the miracle itself, has been pointed out by Betz (1978:69); but the conclusion is usually clearly stated. A survey of miracle stories in Matthew and Luke[4] establishes the frequency of full narrative closure in this form. Funk (1978:57–95) and Theissen

---

[4] A detailed analysis of miracle stories in the Gospel of Mark will be included in chapter six.

(1983) have explored the formal and structural features of miracle stories and their studies lay out a characteristic framework.[5]

Jesus confronts a person with a need; immediately the reader asks the question, "What will happen to that person?" As a rule the Gospels clearly answer that question in the text. Whether it can be attributed to the demands of the form or to the medical interests of the author of the third gospel, Luke's miracle stories achieve full and clear closure:

> Now Simon's mother-in-law was ill with a high fever and they besought him for her. And he stood over her and rebuked the fever, and it left her; and immediately she rose and served them (Luke 4:38b–39).

A person has a need, the need is brought to Jesus' attention, he acts in association with a verbal command, and the healing is described. This pattern persists throughout the third gospel.[6]

Matthew also customarily rounds off his accounts of healing miracles with some statement and proof of good health: "his leprosy was cleansed" (8:3); "the servant was healed" (8:13); "he rose and went home" (9:7); "the woman was made well" (9:22); and "the girl arose" (9:25).[7] Sandwiched among these examples, Matthew 8:28–34 is a notable exception. When Jesus arrives in Gadara he is confronted by two demoniacs; their violent tendencies and hostile words are described and quoted. We have a clear picture of their state and therefore their needs. At Jesus' word the demons enter some pigs, the pigs rush into the sea and drown, and the herdsmen flee in terror. The townspeople come out to see Jesus and beg him to leave, which he does. But what happened to the demoniacs? The only mention of the subjects of the story is contained in the vague reference to the herdsmen's report of "what happened to the demoniacs." A main focus of the story, those with need, has disappeared. We assume by implication that since the demons "came out" the demoniacs are now in their right mind (A1, 3). Even stories so given to closure as miracle stories may force (or invite) the reader to supply the final information regarding the state of the stricken character.

---

[5] See also reviews of Theissen by H. Boers and P. Achtemeier in *Semeia* 11.

[6] See also Luke 4:35, 5:13, 25; 7:10, 15; 8:47, 55; 9:42; 10:13; 14:4; 17:14; and 18:43.

[7] See also Matthew 9:30, 33; 12:13; 22; 15:28; and 17:18.

Encounter stories. Stories of Jesus' personal encounters with a variety of people characterize John's gospel. These stories are in turn characterized by suspended endings. John's tendency is to supply a narrative framework that is never completed. The words of Jesus so totally dominate the conclusions that at times the narrative features of the story barely or never re-emerge. The story of Nicodemus (John 3:1–21) begins with the details of setting and character; a respected Pharisee comes secretly to Jesus with serious spiritual questions. But conversation turns to monologue (v. 10) and monologue may evolve into editorial interpretation (v. 16). A return to the characters, the questions, the narrative setting is never actualized. There is no recorded answer, no response by Nicodemus to the description of God's love or the Son's sacrifice, no faith or rejection described in the conclusion (A3). The effect which John seems to have desired by suspending the narrative ending of the incident (and the effect that has certainly been felt by a great many readers) is the substitution of the reader into the unfilled place of Nicodemus at the end of the narrative. The question "How did he respond?" merges with "How would one respond" to become "How would I respond?"

The story of Jesus' encounter with a Samaritan woman (John 4:1–42) achieves some closure but much remains unfulfilled. In a wide-ranging discussion of personal and theological issues Jesus guides the woman to a confrontation with herself and with him. She rushes back to town and leads the townspeople out to see this one who may be the Messiah. They believe; but what of the woman? The fact that she left her jar unclaimed, her water undrawn, the promised drink unprovided, we basically ignore. But does she believe and what does she believe? On the basis of a suggestive question ("Can this be the Christ?") and on the basis of the ending that is there ("Many Samaritans believed in him because of the woman's testimony") we supply an ending that is not there—an at least fledgling faith in Jesus as Messiah and Savior (B1b).

The story of the raising of Lazarus (John 11) is interesting for the way it focuses on the pleading of Mary and Martha and the death and raising of their brother Lazarus and then forgets them completely. Of their reaction, their emotions, their joy, their amazement, their faith, we know nothing but assume everything. The only reaction we learn of is that of the Jews, some of whom believe in Jesus as a result of the resurrection, others of whom file a report with the authorities.[8] But not only is a description of their emotional reaction excluded; there is no description of what these main characters (even Lazarus) do after Jesus' words "Unbind him, and let him go." That command stands for a whole series of actions which we naturally read out of and into the ending of the story (B1c).

Pronouncement stories. Semeia 20 demonstrates that paradigms, apophthegms, or pronouncement stories are highly structured; but they are also notoriously open-ended. They are by definition stories in which a narrative framework serves only to introduce a saying of Jesus which supplants narrative closure. All pronouncement stories have suspended endings in the sense that the saying replaces the setting; but some tell enough of a story that unanswered questions remain after the pronouncement is made. When Pharisees complained that his disciples were working on the Sabbath by plucking grain (Mark 2:23–28), Jesus announced that the Sabbath was made for man and that he was Lord of the Sabbath. Did the disciples go on eating or not? When Jesus' family tried to see him (and take him home?) one day (Mark 3:31–35), he taught the crowd about the basis for true spiritual relatedness. Did he go out to his family? Did they enter? Did they go away? When three potential disciples approach Jesus about following him (Luke 9:57–62), he reminds them of the cost of such a commitment. Were they discouraged or challenged? Did they turn away or follow more eagerly? In each case[9] we do not know the narrative, only the didactic, conclusion. A pronouncement replaces and in a sense stands for the rest of the story. The fact that we focus on the saying does not mean we forget the story; we provisionally fill in the suspended ending in one way or another at least partially on the basis of the pronouncement. The disciples stopped eating but only because their hunger abated, not because the Pharisees said to. Or they continued to eat under the protection of Jesus' pronouncement. The family went away jealous and rejected by Jesus' broader definition and experience of family. Or they contacted him on the terms of his own views.

---

[8] This story supplies some suggestive parallels with the ending of Mark. Before the resurrection we perceive a mixture of faith (vv. 22, 27) and misunderstanding (vv. 24, 39). After the raising we hear and see nothing of sisters and brothers. No interpreter assumes that the silence signifies loss of faith or a lack of faith. The truncated narrative is no evidence of failure.

[9] Compare also Mark 6:1–4; Matthew 10:13–15; and Matthew 22:15–22.

The inquirers either left or followed, but whichever, on the basis of Jesus' expectations. However we interpret the narrative ending that is not there, we do so in the light of the discursive ending which is there (Blc).

Parables. The recognition of unresolved endings in many of Jesus' parables is a commonplace of New Testament interpretation. "There is often no expressed conclusion to the story, and it ends, so to speak, in mid-air. We are not given nicely rounded and completed tales".[10] Less often observed is the functional role silence plays in the meaning-structure of parables. In summarizing his analysis of several parables, Breech (1983:221) observes,

> We have also seen that silence functions internally in every one of Jesus' core parables, for their meaning emerges in terms of what is said against the back ground of what is not said; in other words, silence plays an important role in the creation of meaning within each narrative.

These two observations unite in the analysis of the meaning-effect of silences at the conclusion of parables. That analysis must include the illustration of the open-endedness of many parables, the illustration of the meaning-effect of silences in parables, and most importantly the identification of the ways in which silences, especially suspended endings, create meanings.

Many parables, of course, achieve full closure. The parable of the Sower (or more appropriately the Four Soils) (Matthew 13:3–8) moves from sowing to harvest, from seed to fruit. The growth of some of the seeds may be thwarted but the story progresses without hindrance to its natural, stated conclusion. At times, however, parables which seem to reach a clear resolution involve unresolved elements on other levels. The parable of the wise and foolish maidens (Matthew 25: 1–13) moves from the original setting (the girls going to the banquet), to the crisis situation (five girls running out of oil), to the conclusion (five included and five excluded from the banquet). But what of the banquet, the goal of the narrative? What did those admitted experience and what happened to those turned away? These questions may not be central to the meaning of the parable but neither are they idle, either literarily or theologically.

---

[10] Barclay: 75; other texts which offer helpful literary perspectives on the parables include Wilder, *Early Christian Rhetoric* (1964) and Funk, *Language, Hermeneutics, and the Word of God* (1966).

When "the door was shut" to the great wedding feast, the mind of the reader is just then opened to the unspoken implications of the actions of the girls (A1).

In some parables the story is simply never concluded; one incident occurs which looms large and overwhelms the story, blocking any possibility of, perhaps any need for, an ending. The whole purpose of the story in Matthew 22:2–13 is again a wedding feast. But the feast never takes place. After the invited guests refuse to attend, a rag-tag bunch has at last been assembled; but then one guest improperly dressed has to be expelled from the hall. There the parable ends, while we wonder what might happen at the as-yet-to-be-celebrated feast (A). Our attention is still fixed on the elements of absence in the story—those who would not come and the one who could not stay. In other parables the story is concluded but in a way that does not answer all the questions which the narrative poses. In Luke 16:1–8a, the dishonest steward is about to be relieved of his position. He quickly and shrewdly closes out some accounts in a way which makes a profit for his master and friends for himself. But the last statement in the story ("The master commended the dishonest steward for his prudence") is a mild reversal (cp. v. 2) and leaves us with a number of questions (A3). What did he say? Did he flatter but still fire? Did he merely reassign him to a less responsible post? Or did he reinstate him because of his prudence?

A number of parables end without narrative closure but with an instructional statement or question which replaces and suggests a conclusion. The parable of the weeds in the wheat (Matthew 13:24–30) tells a straightforward story. A man sows wheat in a field. His enemies secretly sow weeds among the wheat. When the seeds sprout, the servants discover the mixed crop and ask the master if he wants them to try to weed the field. The parable ends with his answer: "No; lest in gathering the weeds you root up the wheat along with them. Let both grow together until the harvest; and at harvest time I will tell the reapers, Gather the weeds first and bind them in bundles to be burned, but gather the wheat into my barn." Notice that the action of the story is never completed; the problem has not been resolved when the account ends. Instead an instruction within an instruction, the statement of a future command to perform a future deed, replaces the deed itself (B1c). Discourse stands for and suggests the action. The narrative ends but a command carries the story on to its conclusion in the mind of the reader.

In a similar vein the parable of the talents (Matthew 25:14-30) substitutes commands for narrative conclusion. When each servant reports on his use or non-use of the entrusted money, the master promises either a reward or punishment, neither of which is carried out in the parable. It closes with the words, "Take the talent from him . . . and cast the worthless servant into the outer darkness," and not with the actions they command. But the words are enough: the works are wrought in our minds as surely as if they had been described in the parable (B1c).

A variation on the parable which ends with a command to act rather than the act itself is the parable which ends with a question. Many of Jesus' parables are followed by a question but some have a question as their last integral element. Luke 12:16–20 records the story of a rich man who built even bigger barns to store his surplus crops and looked with confidence to the future, counseling himself to "eat, drink, and be merry." The parable ends with the sudden intervention of a statement and a question from God: "Fool! This night your soul is required of you, and the things you have prepared, whose will they be?" The death has not occurred and does not occur in the narrative even though we know that in the story it must and it will. Instead the reader is left with a question and with questions (B1c). Matthew 21:33–40 supplies another example. A landowner leased a vineyard to some tenants, who mistreated if not killed the representatives of the owner (first servants and finally his son) who came to collect the rent. Then come the words: "When therefore the owner of the vineyard comes, what will he do to those tenants?" Jesus' words slip from conclusion proper to comment on the parable, from suggestion of the next step in the unrelated narrative action to question regarding the final act (B1c). But it is the response of Jesus' audience that becomes interesting at this point: the chief priests and elders not only 1) were able to supply the precise and proper ending which Jesus had intended and implied (v. 41) but also 2) placed themselves into the parable Jesus told and the ending they had appended (v. 45). The process of thinking and speaking the unnarrated ending motivated by Jesus' question aided if not caused their application of the parable to themselves and contributed to the extremity of their reaction (the desire to arrest Jesus, v. 46).

The trio of parables in Luke 15 provides an interesting test case for some of these theories. The Lost Sheep (Luke 15:4–6) tells of a shepherd who daringly leaves a whole flock to rescue one sheep. When he finds it he rejoices and calls together his friends, saying, "Rejoice with me, for I have found my sheep." A command anticipates and actualizes the unnarrated action. We are not told whether they rejoiced or not, although what is narrated—the willingness to gather at his command—makes us certain of the reaction that is not narrated—their willingness to celebrate at his good fortune (B1b, c). The second parable, the Lost Coin (Luke 15:8–9), is structurally identical: a woman with ten coins loses one, finally finds it, and calls together her friends demanding, "Rejoice with me, for I have found the coin which I had lost." Once again we assume they joined the celebration because 1) they joined her at all, and 2) the command to act assumes the action (B1b, c). With the emphasis on the gathering and commanding of the friends and given the historical context in which the stories are set (Luke 15:1–2), it might be more appropriate to call these the parables of the rejoicing friends.

The third parable, the Lost Son (Luke 15:11–32), is a more elaborately told tale which appears to reach full closure. A younger son leaves home to make it on his own, fails, and returns home, preferring slavery in his father's house to freedom anywhere else. The pattern is the classic pattern of the hero-myth: separation, initiation, and reunion. But every ending is a beginning, and this first narrative movement concludes with a commencement: "they began to make merry." These words supply their own sense of mild openness in spite of the mythic rounding off (A1); but, of course, the parable is not over.

The second narrative movement, which corresponds to the calling and commanding of the friends in the first two parables, finds an older son angry over the welcome-home party for his profligate and prodigal brother. He refuses to enter and the parable ends with the father outside begging the older brother to join the celebration. But even the climactic entreaty is implied (the words of the father never directly invite the older brother to enter or commune or rejoice) and the action remains unrecounted. There is even more indirection in this parable than in the others. Not only is the action omitted; even the command to act is implied. On the basis of the reading of the Lost Sheep and the Lost Coin and on the basis of the fairly simple and certain supplementation accomplished at their conclusions, we as readers are able to supply the moral imperative at the conclusion of the Lost Son. Not only do we know what the elder brother should do; we catch ourselves speaking the unspoken words we have been taught to say, "Rejoice with me." On another level, just as the first two parables establish a pattern which helps us fill in the third, so the first narrative movement (the separation, initiation, and return of the younger son) creates an expectation for the reunion which the second narrative movement does not relate (B1, 2).

The parable of the Good Samaritan (Luke 10:30–35) provides confirmation of the ease with which readers can and have read coherence and closure into the texts of New Testament parables which leave a variety of narrative elements, including the ending, unstated. This final example is not only a sample but a model on which to build a way of reading other texts which display similar openness.[11]

Paraenetically, full closure is achieved: a man was harmed, a man was ignored, a man was helped. The inquirer in the narrative framework has no trouble answering the question, "who proved to be the neighbor?" But other questions remain: did the man recover, did he complete his journey, did the Samaritan complete his journey? In short, we are left, at least on one level, still asking the question, "What happened?" An outline of parallel narrative sequences illustrates the various lacunae in the text and demonstrates how the parable itself makes provision for reading the rest of the story.[12]

Suspensions are numerous and varied. Silence as a rhetorical device is demonstrated in 10:32: "So likewise a Levite. . . ." "Likewise" signals that we should mentally repeat the predicate of the previous sentence; the one word carries the weight of "was going down that road." Silence may represent an irrelevant detail. The travel plans of the robbers, unlike those of the other characters, are unknown to us. Silence can suggest more relevant details. At the point of the interruption of the journeys, nothing in the experience of the priest or Levite corresponds to either the emotion or the action found in the experiences of the robbers or the Samaritan. The silent implications (that they felt nothing and did nothing) are as eloquent as any statements to that effect. In the same vein the departure of the religious leaders is so similar to the departure of the

---

[11] The very title which custom has given this parable—the *Good* Samaritan—is testimony that we read information into this story which the narrative itself does not record.

[12] Daniel Patte (1976:35–52) has executed a structural analysis of the parable of the Good Samaritan which highlights some of these same features. Using Proppian functions and the actantial model of Greimas, he has not only isolated the "deep structures" of the text but also illustrated the missing components in the surface structure. My analysis, which moves on the surface level, is independent of Patte's; but considering the differences in method, the results are not dissimilar.

THE GOOD SAMARITAN   LUKE 10:30–35

	I. Man	II. Robbers	III. Priest	IV. Levite	V. Samaritan
A	30) A man	and he fell among robbers,	31) Now by chance a priest	32) So likewise a Levite,	33) But a Samaritan
B	was going down	[ ]	was going down	[likewise]	as he journeyed,
C	from Jerusalem to Jericho,	[ ]	that road;	when he came to that place	came to where he was;
D	and he fell among robbers who stripped him and beat him,	[ ] who stripped him and beat him,	and when he saw him [ ] [ ]	and saw him, [ ] [ ]	and when he saw him he had compassion, and went to him and bound up his wounds pouring on oil and wine; then he set him on his own beast and brought him to an inn, and took care of him.
E	[ ] and departed, leaving him half dead.	and departed, leaving him half dead.	he passed by on the other side.	passing by on the other side.	35) And the next day he took out two denarii and gave them to the innkeeper saying, Take care of him; and whatever more you spend, I will repay you when I come back.

A. Mention of Individual
B. Notice of Journey
C. Limits/Locus of Journey

D. Interruption of Journey
E. Resumption of Journey

robbers that we hear "leaving him half-dead" echoing at the end of each of the next two narrative sequences.

The suspension which is most significant for this study is at the ending. The narrative begins as a journey from Jerusalem to Jericho. The incidents in the story are dramatic insofar as they hinder or help the continuation of that journey. But in the parable the journey is never completed. The parable does not tell us whether or not the hindrance to completion of the journey, the ill health of the traveler, is actually removed. But the parable does provide the information we need to read the outcome of the physical problems and his travels.

First, the mention of the destination (Jericho) creates the expectation of arrival (B1a). Second, the ministration of the Samaritan and the promise of payment for further medical attention are textual anticipations and assurances of a healing which the text does not include (B1b). Third, the Samaritan actually starts the injured man on his journey again; although another pause at the inn interrupts his progress, this interruption will speed rather than slow his arrival at his destination.[13] Fourth, the pattern of other journeys in the narrative is suggestive. Robbers, priests, and Levite all arrive and depart. In the clause "when I come back" we are told (if indirectly) that the Samaritan continued his journey as well. Fifth, this parable includes the common device of a closing exhortation. The instructions of the Samaritan form as it were a commentary on the unnarrated conclusion of the story (B1c).

These observations remind us that we appear to anticipate suspended endings on the basis of three factors: 1) suggestive foreshadowing (the mention of the destination, the ministration of Samaritan and innkeeper, and the journey resumed); 2) suggestive patterning (the continued and completed journeys of other characters, especially the Samaritan); and 3) suggestive ending (the ending that is there, a command, suggesting the ending that is not there, an action).

Suspended Endings in Longer Narratives

Although Mark's conclusion with its textual, grammatical, and narrative peculiarities receives the most attention, Mark is not the

---

[13] Breech: 179; "The third man transcends the situation in order to continue the man's story for him to the conclusion which therefore is not an ending but . . . a commencement."

only book-length narrative in the New Testament with a foreshortened ending. Three of the four Gospels omit the account of the ascension, the event which climaxes any account of the "life of Jesus" built from the "harmonized" gospels. Only Luke gives details of the event whose description is obviously "secondary . . . to its theological meaning" (Robinson: 246). A place for the ascension to have been narrated has been pointed out by commentators of the other gospels: an ascension may be assumed between appearances in Matthew 28 and John 20. But the event is not narrated explicitly. This is all the more significant since the ascension formed one of the foundation stones of the Lucan apostolic kerygma[14] and its description is the opening scene of the narrative of the book of Acts. A brief analysis of the omission of the ascension narrative in Matthew and John and a look at the ending of Acts offers further and final preparation for a reading of the suspended ending of Mark.

Matthew. The ascension of Jesus is not totally ignored in Matthew even though its narration is suspended. There are several references to the return of Jesus from heaven—e.g., "For the Son of Man is to come with his angels in the glory of his Father" (Matthew 16:27)[15]—which create the expectation of a removal from earth (B1b). On the basis of Pauline texts, we assume that the Christian tradition, which had reached most of the readers of Matthew before the gospel itself did, also created the anticipation of such a conclusion to the story of Jesus.

The gospel actually closes with an exhortation, the Great Commission (Matthew 28:18–20). It contains elements which suggest an ascension in the story-future of the account (B1c). First, Jesus declares his authority in heaven, as well as on earth. Second, the commission to travel and teach among all nations implies physical separation from Jesus. And third, the protestation of his spiritual presence is the surest clue to his impending physical absence. How does this story end? We expect and assume an event which allows the closing command of Jesus to make sense.

The ascension is not the only unnarrated event foreshadowed in this gospel and embedded in its conclusion; the ministry of the apostles is assumed although not described. That the author expected the readers to read the carrying out of the commission in the

[14] Acts 2:33–36; 3:20–21; 7:55–60; 9:3–5; 22:6–8; 26:13–15.

[15] See also 24: 30 and 26:64. If as some say Jesus was not referring to himself in these statements, his listeners at least understood that he was: witness the use of the sayings by gospel writers and the reaction of the high priest in 26:65.

commission itself is supported by Matthew 10:1–7. In a commission with many thematic and structural similarities to 28:18–20, Jesus calls the apostles to him, speaks of their delegated authority, and commands them to go to the lost sheep of Israel and preach the kingdom of God. That evangelistic journey is never described. "And when Jesus had finished instructing his twelve disciples, he went from there" (11:1). The disclosure stands for the description; the commission replaces the consummation. In the same way, the second commission at the close of the gospel both anticipates and actualizes the fulfillment of the commission in the mind of the reader (Bla).

Thus we read the ascension and the apostolic ministry in the ending of Matthew on the basis of 1) suggestions from the text which foreshadow such events, 2) a synecdochal reading of 28:18–20 where the discourse stands for the deed, and 3) a structural analogy from 10:1–7.

John. John 6:62 supplies an instructive paradigm of the amply foreshadowed but unnarrated event of the ascension in the gospel of John. The verse includes a protasis without an apodosis: "Then if you were to see the Son of Man ascending where he was before. . . ." The gospel—at least in that aspect of its plot which leads from God to this world and looks back to reunion in a divine realm—is also an unfinished sentence.

John's gospel creates the expectation of an ascension in a different and more direct way than does Matthew. John's prologue (1:1–18) emphasizes both the beginning of the Word and his eternal presence with God. The Divine Word has come into the world (1:9) and "pitched his tent" among us (1:14). Already in the beginning we anticipate what kind of end full closure would involve (Bla). Among the many allusions to the ascension[16] a few stand out: "Jesus knew that his hour had come to depart out of this world to the Father" (13:1); "because I go to my Father and you will see me no more" (16:10); "I have not yet ascended to my Father; but go to my brethren and say to them, I am ascending to my Father" (20:17) (Blb).

References to being "lifted up" and "going to the Father" are, of course, deliberately ambiguous, pointing to the crucifixion and the

---

[16] John 3:13; 6:38, 41, 42, 50, 51, 58; 7:33–34; 8:21–23; 13:3; chapters 14 and 15 passim; 16:28.

resurrection as well as the ascension (Brown: 1013). This paradigmatic connection to the cross and the resurrection is itself a foreshadowing of the ascension. But because the statement in 20:17
comes after the first two events we recognize it as a special and
specific foreshadowing of the ascension. It is also important for
another reason: it is a discourse commanding further discourse
regarding a future event which is never narrated. Jesus tells Mary he
will soon ascend and commands her to tell the disciples this news.
The next verse informs the reader that she carried out her commission, but this double discourse on the ascension is the closest John
comes to the event itself.

Like Matthew, John also makes provision for reading ascension
and mission into the ending of his gospel. "Jesus said, If it is my will
that he remain until I come, what is that to you? Follow me." With
the command "Follow me" a certain amount of closure is reached:
these same words formed Jesus' original call to discipleship (1:40f).
And yet the words open up on a continuing journey, a future of
movement and ministry. The clause "until I come" emphasizes the
far future of the parousia and the reality of the near future, the
ascension which we expect but do not read (Blc).

Acts. The ending of the book of Acts, like that of Mark, has
raised a variety of textual, compositional, and historical questions.
Luke's two-volume work has followed Paul's travels over the last
fourth of its pages. After a series of trials and a dramatic voyage to
Rome, Paul is under house arrest awaiting disposition of the Jewish
charges against him. The book closes with these words: "And he
lived there two whole years at his own expense, and welcomed all
who came to him, preaching the kingdom of God and teaching about
the Lord Jesus Christ quite openly and unhindered" (Acts 28:30–
31).

The textual question involves a weakly attested Western reading
which shifts the emphasis in the conclusion even more than the
accepted text onto the gospel Paul preached: "saying that this is the
Christ, Jesus the Son of God, by whom the whole world is to be
judged."[17] This reading is similar to the interpretation many give to
the ending of Acts: that Luke's interest is in the spread of the gospel
not the fate of Paul and that the promise of the expansion of the

---

[17] Only a few Latin and Vulgate manuscripts and a Syrian edition include the
addition.

gospel in 1:8 has reached a full and fitting climax. Even so Luke is silent on two points in which he and his readers have invested a good deal of attention—the results of Paul's preaching in Rome and the results of Paul's legal appeal. The tantalizing mention of the "two whole years" impels us to ask, "What happened then?"

Some commentators stand with Ramsay (1982:321f) against this ending as the intended conclusion: "No one can accept the ending of *Acts* as the conclusion of a rationally conceived history." These scholars insist that some interruption caused an unnatural conclusion; perhaps a third volume was planned to "finish" the story (Zahn) or Luke died before completing the book (Lietzmann). Others are content to speculate about what really did happen next: the accusers failed to appear so Paul was released, Paul was tried and acquitted, or Paul was tried and executed (Marshall: 425–426).

Still others approach the present conclusion with a more positive literary judgment: Bruce (1966:535) sees the ending as "an impressive and artistic conclusion." But even if this ending is intended or at least coherent, how are we to read it? The first step is to sense its openendedness (A). Acts tells us nothing directly about Paul's fate or further travels, nothing about the church in Rome or the gospel's progress there. The second step is to recognize that by suggestion, synecdoche, and structure, the work may help us make sense of its absent ending (B1). Paul's words in 20:25 ("I know that all you among whom I have gone about preaching the kingdom will see my face no more") can be taken in two ways; either Paul was overly pessimistic and was freed by Roman authorities or Paul's word foreshadowed the death which Luke's conclusion knows but avoids.[18]

The positive, progressive conclusion of Acts seems to militate against the negative foreshadowing of 20:25. Just as Paul's progress has been the gospel's progress, so now we read Paul's fate in the fate of the gospel. The sense of freedom in what is told to us about Paul's two-year detention (28:30–31) may be a "concentrated account" (Marshall: 421) which recapitulates the spread of the gospel in Rome, the strength of the church there, and the success of Paul's appeal.

---

[18] So Goodspeed and Dibelius. Marshall: 426: "Luke was unwilling to record his martyrdom; he had given hints in advance about it, and he preferred to leave his readers with the gospel being freely proclaimed by Paul in Rome." Some argue that Paul was executed but that Luke did not need to make direct reference to his death since Luke's readers, knowing Nero, would have assumed such an outcome; see Bartlett, *Expositor* VIII.v (1913): 464ff.

A third tool for reading the unnarrated ending is structural patterning (B2). Much in the same way as the commissioning discourse in Matthew 10 influenced our reading of Matthew 28:18–20, the conclusion of the first of the two main sections of Acts may aid our interpretation and help us resolve the contradictory signals. The first half of Acts ends with one of Luke's summary statements about the advance of the gospel (12:24). That structural feature, the sixth and last of which is found in Acts 28:31, is immediately preceded by 1) the account of Peter's arrest, imprisonment, release, and removal to another place of ministry (Acts 12:1–17) and 2) the account of the death of Herod Agrippa I, the Jewish king who had been persecuting Peter and his fellow Christians (12:18–23). Other evidence being equal, this parallel suggests that Luke intended for his readers to assume that Paul's release and the removal of the Jewish threat would follow his arrest and imprisonment.

Whether or not this specific reconstruction of the meaning of the ending of Acts can be proven, several points have again been illustrated. A variety of forms in the New Testament are open-ended or close without supplying some of the information the readers anticipated. In this, Mark is not alone. A number of texts in the New Testament display the common device of foreshadowing to create anticipation for a certain conclusion and to aid our intuition of that conclusion when it is, after all, not narrated. Many of the texts, short as well as long, are written so as to give structural clues to the intended but suspended ending. And many of these texts end in such a way that, under the influence of suggestive foreshadowing and structural patterning, the reader may read the ending that is not there in the ending that is there. Just as other New Testament texts share some of the characteristics of Mark's odd ending, so will the analysis of the ending of Mark depend on these approaches which have proved helpful in interpreting the ending of other New Testament texts.

CHAPTER VI

"NOTHING TO NO ONE": STRUCTURE AND SILENCE IN MARK

> 22. Let no one say that I have said nothing new; the arrangement of the subject is new.
> 23. Words differently arranged have a different meaning, and meanings differently arranged have different effects.
>
> —Pascal[1]

Textual criticism of the Gospel of Mark has revealed that the work closes with a sudden silence, the suspension of the expected narration of a confirming reappearance of the crucified and risen Jesus. Some literary critics and many theologians affirm that this silence is also significant, meaningful in itself and in its effect. The task remains to interpret the meaning of that ending. It has often been claimed that the attempt to interpret an absent ending is an enterprise appropriate only to modern literature. On the contrary, the preceding chapters have demonstrated that ancient literature abounds with open or suspended endings and provides some effective guidelines for a credible interpretation of Mark's conclusion. Three recurring principles are the use of internal suggestions which foreshadow unnarrated conclusions; the use of structural patterns which prepare us to read an "empty" structure at the end; and the use of synecdoche, an element narrated at the close of the text which implies by substitution or analogy the suspended ending of the story. We turn in this chapter to the second of these points, the relationship of the overall structure and smaller structures of the Gospel of Mark to its ending.

The analysis necessarily involves two aspects. First, the ending

---

[1] The *Pensees* of Blaise Pascal (1952:175) demonstrates a sensitivity both to literary and theological matters; there is also a fascinating exploration of the topics of structure and silence.

must be read in the light of the overall structure. Commenting on the ending of the *Odyssey*, Bury (1922:9) writes, "In considering a question of this kind, account must be taken of the general scheme of the composition of the book." The theory of readerly activity teaches us that silences have meaning, indeed may be given meaning, by means of the language structures around them: "if blanks open up this network of possible connections, there must be an underlying structure regulating the way in which segments determine each other" (Iser: 196). Just as the content of literary communication is expressed structurally, so the potentialities, the gaps, the silences, must be implied structurally. Thus this chapter first explores the structure of Mark in an attempt to explain the openness and to give shape to its suspended elements—in short, to explain what is not there.

Second, the ending must be read in the light of smaller structures within the text. The paradigmatic comparison of elements in stories from the same genre has been a fruitful procedure ever since Propp's work (1968) with Russian fairy stories. But paradigmatic models are helpful in interpretive studies as well as comparative ones. Repeated structures not only generate other structures; they also help us read meaningfully the silences in the skeletal structures. This process operates in the Bible as well as in other literature.

> Recurrences, parallels, analogy are the hallmark of reported action in the biblical tale. The use of narrative analogy, where one part of the story provides a commentary on or a foil to another, would be familiar enough from later literature. . . . In the Bible, however, such analogies often play an especially critical role because the writers tend to avoid more explicit modes of conveying evaluation of particular characters and acts (Alter: 180).

Thus this chapter will finally explore these smaller structures, the miracle stories and other shorter narrative units, which function as (in Alter's terms) "type-scenes" for the scene at the end of Mark—in short, to explain what is there.

The Structure of the Gospel of Mark

Any interpretation of 16:1-8 must take into account the whole structure of the Gospel of Mark. To put it simply, no part of a literary work is independent of the rest of the work. Aristotle taught us to recognize the relationship of the beginning, the middle, and the end. Modern literary critics have taught us to read the end in the beginning and the beginning in the end. So we expect to learn something about the conclusion from the work which precedes it. The whole Gospel, from first to last, points to 16:1–8, especially to 16:7 (Marxsen: 91–92).

The Gospel has been outlined on the basis of a variety of perspectives. A geographical orientation emphasizes the sites of Jesus' ministry, Galilee (1:14-9:50) and Jerusalem (10:1–15:47) (Grant: 636). Emphasis on the character of Jesus suggests a division at 8:30. The first half of the book reveals Jesus as the Messianic Son of God, the authoritative Christ, climaxed with the confession of Peter. The second half exhibits Jesus in terms of the suffering Son of Man, the crucified one, climaxed with the testimony of the centurion.[2] Other outlines focus on the disciples or the reaction of secondary characters to the figure of Jesus. Weeden's outline, for instance, emphasizes the attitude of the disciples: 1:16–8:26, imperception of the disciples; 8:27–14:9, misconception of the disciples; 14:10–72, rejection of the disciples (1968:145–148). But as helpful as outlines are, they frequently are imposed on the basis of limited perspectives or theological presuppositions. The literary structure of Mark supplies its own outline.

The ending of the Gospel of Mark is, in a sense, a reflection of the beginning of the Gospel, its title (1:1) and its prologue (1:2–13); and the ending can be read in the beginning. The abruptness of the ending is no more scandalous than the abruptness of the beginning.[3] In fact, T. W. Manson insists that the original beginning of Mark is the missing element.[4] Unlike the other canonical gospels there is not a word about Jesus' origins, human or divine. He is declared (by the narrator) to be the son of God and Messiah, but no royal genealogies or miraculous birth accounts introduce the hero's exploits or confirm the claims to divinity, as in Matthew and Luke. The testimony of John the Baptist in Mark makes it clear that Jesus is one come from God; and yet there is no statement, let alone description, of the divine incarnation as in the Gospel of John.

But brevity is not the only factor which the beginning and the end have in common. In Mark's introduction, *euangelion* ("good

---

[2] This material is derived from the outline of E. Schweizer (1967), in Kealy (1982:187); see also Rhoads and Michie: 48.

[3] "But really, the brevity of this ending is quite parallel to the beginning of the Gospel" (Gould: 304); "Its abrupt ending is matched by an even more abrupt beginning" (Evans, in Kealy: 201; see also Lane: 591–592).

[4] Manson relies on syntactical evidence: the absence of a predicate in v. 1 and the absence of a main clause in vv. 2–3 (Kealy: 174).

news") is the content and the conveyance is an *angelos* ("messenger" or "angel"), or rather a series of *angeloi*. Mark the narrator-angelos quotes Isaiah the prophet-angelos, speaking for God regarding another prophet-angelos (John) who will prepare the way for the Lord. The Messiah will follow this forerunner. The prophetic sequence of revelation, proclamation, and action is firmly established. At the conclusion, the narrator-angelos reports on a young man-angelos, reminding the women of Jesus' own words and charging them to serve as angeloi to the disciples regarding the future actions of Jesus. The disciples will follow the Messiah, and the prophetic sequence of revelation, proclamation, and action is duplicated.

Thus Mark begins as he ends, having lopped off what inevitably lies behind the point at which he begins and what inevitably follows the point at which his text stops. He begins as he ends, having raised and lowered the curtain with Jesus off-stage, but present in revelation, proclamation, and responsive action. He begins as he ends, omitting an event (first Jesus' appearance, then his reappearance) on which the sense of the Gospel depends, focusing on an angelos (first a man in camel's hair clothing, then a man in white shining clothes), promising a proclamation of the good news concerning the revealed and at last resurrected Son of God (first by a prophetic forerunner, then by fearful but faithful followers). The comparative structures of the framework of this Gospel, the prologue of 1:1–13 and the epilogue of 16:1–8, indicate that readers would naturally expect proclamation to follow the announcement of the good news by the women just as it had followed the original prophetic pronouncements by John in chapter one.

Just as the beginning of the Gospel foreshadows and fore-shapes the last scene, so the major sections of the Gospel anticipate the conclusion. Schweizer (1978:389, 399) sees three main sub-sections in the first half of the book. Each section begins with a call to follow; but the first features Jesus' rejection by authorities (1:1–3:6), the second rejection by fellow citizens (3:7–6:6), and the third rejection by the disciples (6:7–8:30). But the rest of the Gospel is not the picture of utter failure by the disciples; instruction, revelation, proclamation, and action fill the succeeding relationships of Jesus and his followers. If this structural pattern holds true, the prophetic proclamation should overcome the temporary rejection; speech should succeed silence; and mission should follow flight.

Perrin (1982) points out another way in which the whole structure suggests a certain ending. Each major section ends on a note which looks forward to the passion. Chapter three, verse six, closes with the plot of the Pharisees and Herodians to destroy the miracle worker. Rejection by his family and friends in Nazareth characterizes the section 3:7–6:6. The third section, 6:7–8:30, describes the misunderstanding of the disciples and lays the groundwork for the first straightforward prediction of his death. Jesus' realization that he is about to "give his life as a ransom for many" closes the passage 8:31–10:45. Open predictions by Jesus and accelerated plotting by his adversaries characterize 10:46–12:44.

The close of the book is also the close of the final section of the book and follows the pattern seen throughout. The suspension of the stories about the reappearance of Jesus, the decision to close at the empty tomb, accomplishes precisely what the other sections accomplish, a focus on the passion. From this perspective the focus on the passion must be a backward glance. Even more effectively than the anticipatory conclusions of the earlier sections, this conclusion retroactively reasserts the testimony of the centurion at the crucifixion with a new significance expressed in the proclamation about the risen Lord. The empty tomb reinterprets the empty cross as a symbol of life not death. By narrating appearance stories Mark would surely not have undermined the importance of the crucifixion; the crucifixion is communicated in all its power and pathos and purpose in the Gospels which do relate post-resurrection appearances. But their absence in Mark stresses the starkness and significance of the death of Jesus in a way not felt in other accounts.

Just as Mark 16:1–8 is similar to the conclusion of the other major sections of the Gospel in its reflexive focus on the passion, so this paradigmatic relationship leads us to expect some forward thrust. The main forward-looking feature of 16:1–8 is verse seven, the promise of reappearance and reunion. By excluding these events Mark satisfies the pattern he has created by maintaining his focus on the passion and a future orientation now on the risen Lord. Thus the suspended ending and the sparse but powerful prologue to the Gospel complement and balance one another and the major sections of the Gospel, climaxed by 16:1–8, reduplicate and reinforce one another.

The Structure of Marcan Miracle Stories

Just as the overall structure of Mark illuminates the meaning of its conclusion, so the many miracle stories in Mark reveal a paradigm which is helpful for interpreting Mark's handling of the resurrection. The interrelationship is three-fold:

1) the empty tomb story, Mark's conclusion, accomplishes the

same purpose as the whole Gospel—to highlight the significance of the passion;

2) the empty tomb story can be compared to other Marcan miracle stories because the resurrection of Jesus is "the central miracle of the Gospel" (Brown: 226); and

3) the miracle stories are the Gospel in miniature, smaller narratives which reduplicate the whole. To ask, therefore, the purpose of Mark's truncated account of the resurrection is to ask the purpose of the miracle stories and to ask the purpose of the whole Gospel. Theissen's answer (1983:213) is suggestive: "The whole of Mark's gospel pushes toward acclamation, toward recognition of Jesus' true status." The issue for Mark is not so much apologetics as it is acclamation, not so much proof as proclamation. If Theissen is right about Mark's program and if we are right about the integral relationship among Gospel, miracle story, and resurrection account, then not only will an analysis of the structure of miracle stories elucidate the structure of 16:1–8 but the way in which Mark realizes his purpose in miracle stories will also educate us to read Mark's intended purpose in his controversial conclusion.

The pattern which miracle stories assume is related to the purpose for which they are told: "The point of miracle stories is the miracle, and based on this the recognition of the revelation which has taken place in the miracle in wonder and acclamation (Theissen: 212). The purpose demands at least four elements in the pattern:

1) a miracle, a (marvelous) thing done, a factum;

2) a recognition, a realization that something (or someone) has been revealed in the deed;

3) a reaction of wonder, a seemingly involuntary amazement in the light of what (or who) was revealed; and

4) a response of acclamation, the voluntary statement of conviction or attestation elicited by the factum and the revelation.

Trompf (1972:319) also recognizes an identifiable format in what he (following the terminology of the form-critics) calls *Novellen*. After characters are introduced and their actions or intentions expressed, there is a "happening" which suggests the agency of spiritual forces. The event results in expressions of fear or related emotions. Divine words ("Come out of him") and/or divine actions (for instance, physical touch) usually by Jesus follow. The conclusion may include an expression of a numinous feeling by the onlookers or a statement of instruction or command by Jesus. Trompf's analysis emphasizes the actions of Jesus toward his audience rather than the

reactions of the audience toward Jesus (Weeden) or the acclamation
of Jesus by his audience (Theissen); but he does add the helpful
observation that two separate waves of emotion—of amazement or
wonder or terror—sweep over the participants in the midst of most
miracle stories.

The emerging pattern is not unlike a structure which Culley
(1976:59–61) has identified in Old Testament miracle stories. Working mainly from the book of Judges, he indicates that commonly a
messenger appears announcing God's intention and plan to save
Israel. Tokens of reverence (offerings or sacrifices) are brought. The
miracle occurs. The response of those who called on God for miraculous assistance is recognition and deeper reverence: they recognize
the messenger as one who acts on the authority of YHWH and they
express their own fear of death at the demonstration of such awe-
some power. At last they are reassured that they have nothing to
fear.

These paradigms are helpful. Theissen's lengthy and detailed
list of structural functions is especially significant (1983:48f). But we
will work from a paradigm both shorter than Theissen's and slightly
different than the many suggestive outlines. It is shorter and it
differs because it focuses on the reaction of the participants rather
than on the actions of Jesus. This course is demanded by the nature
of the ending of Mark and the issues it raises; the meaning of the
responses of the women and the absence of any narrative of further
actions are the questions at the heart of the ongoing debate surrounding 16:1–8.

Five key functions characterize Marcan miracle stories. First,
there is fear, a reaction motivated by confrontation with a situation
which is unknown, uncontrollable, or unsolvable. It is a fear born of
ignorance and helplessness in the presence of some force or need or
want beyond human control or satisfaction. Second, there is recognition, confrontation with Jesus and the identification of him as the
personification of divine power, the one who can act and overcome
human inertia. The statement of recognition might be a cry for help,
an expression of trust, or a declaration of faith; in any case, Jesus has
been revealed and recognized as the one who can alleviate the
situation. Third, there is the factum, the thing done, the miracle
itself. The one who can (it is believed) act does act. The force is
faced, the evil expelled, the illness eased, the need met, the lack
fulfilled. This function is certainly the pivotal one but in Mark's
narrative it may not be the focal one.

Fourth, fear, fear on a new level, emerges. It may be expressed in the text psychologically as amazement or fear or astonishment; it may be expressed physically as trembling or flight. But it is a different kind of fear from the first. This fear$_2$ is based on knowledge and sight, born of trust and elicited by an observed action of rescue. It is not fear of the uncontrollable but fear of the one who can control the uncontrollable (and, therefore, is even more uncontrollable.) It is no longer fear of an incomprehensibly chaotic condition but fear of the power which brings order out of chaos. It is a positive fear, just as powerful as the first fear but more positive. And just as the former fear motivates an expression of need or want or helplessness or despair, so the latter fear motivates its own expression. Thus the fifth function is proclamation. The proclamation may be the full rehearsal of the miracle or a confession of faith in the one who effected it or a statement of joy at the turn of events. The proclamation function may be expressed in its stifling, the command not to proclaim or the inability to proclaim. Then again the proclamation may come in spite of a command to silence or in the midst of great fear. In any case, some such response habitually occurs.

A survey of miracle stories in Mark provides examples of these five functions and fills out the various ways in which Mark brings them to expression. Mark 1:21–28 supplies a clear example from early in Mark's narrative. After describing the setting in place and time, Mark reports on the astonishment (fear$_1$) of the people at an authoritative style and content of teaching which they have never before experienced. Onto the scene bursts a man with an unclean spirit who confronts Jesus and identifies him as the "Holy One of God" (recognition). Jesus rebukes the spirit and calls him forth out of the man (factum). This demonstration of power calls forth deeper and wider astonishment focused on Jesus as the source of miraculous power (fear$_2$). The news about the person of Jesus spreads rapidly throughout Galilee (proclamation).

In 1:32–34 the functions of fear do not surface but the appearance of the other three functions offers an interesting insight. Confronted with disease and possessed neighbors, the townspeople of Capernaum bring those in need to Jesus whom they have perceived as the one who can act where they cannot (recognition). "He healed many who were sick . . . and cast out many demons" (factum). A command to silence directed toward the demons implies their intention to do something like the man with the unclean spirit had done—proclaim to all the identity of Jesus (proclamation). This is borne out by the explanatory clause, "because they knew him." The clause reveals two things. First, at least for Mark, Jesus' identity is the important fact brought to light by the deed and is the issue in proclamation or silence. Second, at least for Mark, silence is a function of knowledge not ignorance, understanding not misunderstanding. They are (should be) silent precisely because they know intuitively and have had confirmed experientially that Jesus of Nazareth is the powerful Son of God.

In 1:40–45 a leper is confronted with his own uncontrollable disease ($fear_1$). He seeks out Jesus, trusting his ability to heal what no one else could (recognition). Jesus heals the man at a touch (factum). The man's emotional reaction ($fear_2$) is not described; but the discussion about his proclamation is described in detail. Jesus warned him to keep silence; the language is severe ("sternly charged") and seemingly absolute ("say nothing to anyone"). But Jesus' own words demonstrate that his absolute prohibition was not meant to be absolute at all: show yourself to the priest as a testimony to them (the ambiguous "them" could refer to the priests or the people or both). Jesus' command to silence and what we assume was the man's obedient silence were not absolute; they were based on appropriateness of person and appropriateness of time. The proclamation must be to the priest, the one whose responsibilities included ritual purification of lepers after their healing. It must be to the priest first, because only then could the act be verified and legitimately announced to the people.

Chapter 2:1–12 describes how four men overcame the barriers of a pressing crowd and well-built roof to gain access to Jesus for their paralyzed friend. Their sense of helplessness in the face of an incurable ailment was matched by their faith in Jesus' ability to meet the need ($fear_1$ and recognition). When Jesus forgives the man, religious leaders give tacit if negative testimony to his identity by pointing out that only God can forgive sins (recognition). Jesus heals the palsied man (factum), whereupon the crowds were amazed ($fear_2$) and glorified God, professing their amazement of what they had observed (proclamation).

Mark 3:7–12 reports the common procedure when Jesus exorcized unclean spirits. When Jesus confronted the subjects, the demons recognized him and identified him as the Son of God. His order to the spirits not to make him known implies that their silence was a function of their knowledge of his identity and power.

A nature miracle in 4:35–41 follows much the same pattern. The disciples fear the presence of a "great storm of wind," a physical calamity over which the sailors have no control in their tiny fishing boat (fear$_1$). These seasoned seamen appeal to the sleeping Jesus to rescue them from the storm (recognition). At a word Jesus stills the storm (factum). It is in the midst of that great physical calm that Mark describes the rising of a great psychological storm, an awe which overtakes the disciples who have been confronted with a person and a power and a demonstration of that power (fear$_2$). And yet their incredulous question is also a testimony of faith: "Who then is this, that even the wind and sea obey him?" (proclamation).

The most dramatic and detailed account of the healing of a demon-possessed man comes in 5:1–20. There a whole town and region fear the uncontrolled ragings of a demoniac (fear$_1$). All attempts to restrain him have failed and he lives a life of crazed self-abuse in some burial caves outside of the town. When Jesus confronts him, the possessed man quickly identifies him as the Son of the Most High God (recognition). After Jesus expels the demons (factum), after the healing has taken place, after the man is sitting, clothed, and in his right mind, after order has been restored—the townspeople are terrified ("and they were afraid") (fear$_2$). Their fear is the reaction of people who have witnessed the evidence of what they take to be super-natural power. Their fear is focused on the person by whose agency the miracle occurred. Finding no other way to handle their fear, they ask him to leave their area. Before he leaves, Jesus commissions the ex-demoniac to tell his friends—not everyone, not the confused townspeople, but his friends—what has taken place (proclamation). Mark declares that the man's testimony occasioned widespread amazement.

Mark 5:21–43 records one healing miracle framed by another. A man troubled by his daughter's approaching death (fear$_1$) seeks out Jesus, trusting that he can preserve her from death (recognition). After a brief but interrupted journey, Jesus reaches the house where they find the girl dead. Jesus raises her from the dead (factum). It is then that the family and friends are "overcome with amazement" (fear$_2$). Contrary to the instructions he gave to the healed demoniac in the story immediately preceding this one (5:1–20), Jesus orders silence so that no one else would know what they knew (non-proclamation). Two things must be noted. First, silence is not representative of misunderstanding but of understanding which must not at this point or to this audience be widely shared. Second, even the most naive readers must realize that they are reading the account of an incident that must have been reported (contrary to the command of Jesus and exclusive of any clear statement in the text) before it could have been recorded (proclamation).

Sandwiched in the midst of this account is the companion healing of a woman utterly frustrated by her chronic menstrual malady and the medical profession's inability to heal her (fear$_1$). Trusting Jesus' power to heal (recognition) she touches him and is healed (factum). When Jesus realizes what has happened and insists on identifying the beneficiary of the miracle, she steps forward "knowing what had been done to her," and yet "in fear and trembling" (fear$_2$). The fear does not signify a lack of faith: "your faith has made you well." The trembling does not imply a lack of trust: "If I touch even his garments, I shall be made well." The (psychological) fear and the (physical) trembling are founded on a knowledge of what has happened. The only proclamation we know of is her rehearsal to Jesus and the listening crowd of the whole incident.

A second prominent nature miracle involves another storm at sea (6:45–51). The disciples are helpless against a strong, contrary wind (fear$_1$). Jesus comes walking on the water toward them and they recognize him, but according to Mark think him a ghost (recognition). When they see him they are terrified. Jesus stills the storm and joins them in the boat (factum). At that point they are utterly astonished (fear$_2$). Mark next injects the first direct notice that misunderstanding accompanies their fear. It may be that Mark expected that their level of amazement would have declined after seeing so many convincing miracles; in spite of the fact that some amazement inevitably accompanies wondrous events, the narrator definitely makes a negative assessment of their bewilderment. On the other hand, it may be that Mark means to connect their misunderstanding to the failure of recognition during the storm rather than a failure to appreciate the miracle and reverence the miracle worker after the storm. This interpretation is certainly more consistent with the Marcan pattern which expects a crisis of identification before the factum and intelligent fear afterwards.

Astonishment, silence, and proclamation are also key elements in 7:31–37. A deaf and mute man is healed by Jesus (factum). Jesus charged those nearby to tell no one else, but "the more he charged them, the more zealously they proclaimed it" (proclamation). General amazement followed the report of the healing (fear$_2$). Once again we see the far from simple relationship of silence and speech. For whatever reason Jesus admonished them not to spread the word and however absolutely he meant the "no one" of his prohibition, proclamation emerged from the command to silence and astonishment emerged from proclamation.

The "resurrection" account of 16:1–8 follows the pattern of the other miracle stories in a muted allusive way. A brief look at that story in the light of the paradigm must precede an attempt at interpretation. The women come to the tomb distressed by the presence of a large stone, an obstacle over which they have no power, an object which stands in the way of their intended anointing of Jesus' body (fear$_1$). The stone is gone, but a young man is there; he identifies Jesus as the one who was buried there but is now risen and gone from the tomb. This narrated dialogue functions as the statement of recognition and serves as the report of the factum, the miracle of the resurrection from the dead. The young man (angel) instructs the women to relay this news to Peter and the other disciples (proclamation). After this uninterrupted sequence of identification, explanation, and command, Mark describes the psychological and physical reactions of the women: they are afraid, they flee the tomb, and they are silent (fear$_2$).

What have the surveys of miracles stories in Mark taught us about these recurring functions?

1) Commands to silence and silences are not necessarily absolute in intention or result, even when the language of the command or report sounds absolute. First, the reference to silence may apply only to a certain aspect of the incident. "In Mark 1:25 the intention is not to keep secret the supernatural status betrayed by the demons; the whole scene is public. The command to be silent is aimed at the apotropaeic power of miraculous knowledge, not against its manifestation" (Theissen: 144). In 1:40f the cleansed leper may be expected to be silent about the circumstances of his healing but not his purification; Jesus may want him to keep quiet about the identity of the healer but not necessarily about the healing. Second, references to silence may apply only to certain periods of time. A delay in proclamation seems to be implied when the target groups—priests (1:43) or friends at home (5:19)—are at some distance. Third, the silence function may refer only to a certain specific audience.

2) In connection with this last point, there appear to be two levels on which the proclamation/non-proclamation construct operates. Indiscriminate proclamation is discouraged by Jesus; discriminate proclamation, proclamation to the appropriate audience, is frequently commanded, and perhaps never ruled out even by the

commands to silence. Thus silence and speech are two equally appropriate responses to the phenomenon of miracle. They are not mutually exclusive even in the same setting.

3) Silence is not necessarily a result of ignorance or misunderstanding; it is a function of knowledge. Silence may be maintained because of awe for Jesus' person and power, or silence may be enjoined precisely because of full knowledge about Jesus' identity (as in the exorcism stories).

4) Fear is an appropriate response to the display or the report of the display of divine power. Whether expressed in terms of amazement, astonishment, or fear, this strong emotional response is characteristic of the reaction of recipients and onlookers in Mark's miracle stories.

5) Trembling is an occasional response to the miraculous in Mark, the physical manifestation of its psychological counterpart, fear.

6) Fear and proclamation are not mutually exclusive. Theissen (1983) may or may not have meant to imply that they are in his statement, "Wonder and acclamation, however, inevitably form a contrast." The fact is that on a number of occasions Mark describes people as responding with both fear and proclamation. In 2:1–12 the crowd is amazed and glorifies God verbally. In 4:35–41 the disciples are filled with awe but speak to each other about their master's power. Mark 5:21–43 records how the woman was overcome with fear and trembling but told Jesus and the onlookers all about what had occurred. And in 7:31–37 the men who brought the deaf-mute to be healed by Jesus were astonished but in their astonishment declared the power of Jesus.

7) A final observation has not surfaced in the preceding summaries of the miracle stories; but it is an important aspect of the Marcan miracle stories and has important implications for our interpretation of 16:1–8. The closing proclamation is often reported but rarely quoted. And when words are quoted they are statements of Jesus' identity. Such statements appear in the recognition section of the story: "What have you to do with me, Jesus, Son of the Most High God?" The very feature which miracle stories seem to be driving toward—the full expression of the identity of Jesus in the light of his miraculous activity and in the context of a fear born of faith and trained by factum—is never realized in the text.

Theissen (1983:162, 173, 214) attributes this omission of the proclamation to the fact that the acclamations, expressions of wonder, statements of faith, were "part of the oral framework" in which these miracle stories were originally recited in the early church. Story tellers and later the evangelists "suppressed" the climactic "christological acclamations," keeping them "latent in the structure" of the miracle story, because they were an inherent part of the audience's reaction to the miracle and the narration of the miracle.

That Mark fits the overall structural paradigm of the Marcan miracle stories has already been observed. The suspended conclusion of Mark must now be analyzed in the light of these observations on the generalizations derived from the paradigm. Structural patterning teaches us to read the ending of Mark as a description of appropriate and positive actions on the part of the women and educates us for the process of reading the ending which is not there.

1) The silence of the women is not necessarily absolute. a) Their silence about the circumstances of their experience at the tomb may not have included silence about the fact they had learned. On the other hand, their silence about the understanding or misunderstanding they had regarding the implications of the event for the identity of Jesus need not have carried with it silence about the incident itself. b) Their immediate awe-struck silence may not have been permanent; they may have said "nothing to anyone" only until, c) passing soliders changing the guard and merchants opening their stalls and shoppers heading for the market, they reached the disciples.

2) As Moule (1965:133) saw, the ending may well imply that they kept silence in the midst of inappropriate audiences but gave a full report to the appropriate audience, the disciples, who were prepared for such news and to whom the women had been commissioned to deliver the news. It is significant that the other story in which those strong words, "nothing to anyone," are found is the healing of the leper where saying *something* to *someone* was specifically commanded and evidently accomplished.

3) Much has been made of the failure of the women and the disciples, the failure to understand and to act. There is no doubt that Mark is open and honest (even to the point of emphasis) about the slowness to perceive, the missed clues, missed meanings, missed opportunities. But Mark's miracle stories teach us that silence either voluntary or commanded is a positive response to heightened knowledge and understanding of Jesus' person and power on the basis of the observation of a demonstration of that supernatural power.

4) The fear of the women is not the ignorant helpless fear they felt when confronted with the closed tomb. Theirs was a higher level fear, educated by observation and instruction. Theirs was the fear which follows a confrontation with order and power. It was motivating fear not debilitating, positive not negative, appropriate to the factum, and therefore reminiscent of the responses of participants in other miracle stories.

5) Trembling accompanied astonishment as the physical response of the women in 16:8. This feature is almost identical to the reaction of the woman in 5:21–43 who proceeded to tell Jesus the whole truth.

6) The note of fear on which the Gospel ends does not in itself rule out the possibility of later proclamation. The fact that future proclamation is not narrated is another matter. We can at least say that fear in miracle stories is often inclusive of praise or proclamation, not exclusive of it.

7) The fact that a clearcut transmission of dialogue regarding Jesus' resurrection and what that means for his identity as the Son of God, i.e., final acclamation, is customarily omitted though assumed at the end of miracle stories may in part explain the strange silence with which the Gospel ends. It may also suggest a positive alternative to the interpretations of fear and silence as failure. That the words of their report to the disciples are not recorded really comes now as no surprise. The statement of Jesus' identity as the crucified, buried, and now risen one in the recognition section (16:6) suffices as it often did in the other stories and suggests the sentiment of the unnarrated final acclamation.

Here lies the possible solution to a central problem: if "The whole of Mark's gospel pushes toward acclamation," towards recognition of Jesus' status (Theissen: 213), why are the women silent about the resurrection and why is Mark silent about post-resurrection appearances? Mark has extended "the arch which is inherent in all the miracle stories to the whole gospel" (Theissen: 215). After having followed recipients and onlookers in miraculous settings who respond with fear and silence and having noted those who are commanded to be silent or to proclaim, "the reader is now aware of the unspoken presence of a titular acclamation" at the end of a miracle story (Theissen: 214). The delay, the suspension of the words of the proclamation, are the paradigmatic signal for the readers to supply the affirmation which has been presaged and presupposed throughout. To have narrated the dialogue of the women with the disciples or to have narrated the reunion of the followers with Jesus would have effectively blocked the completion of the story by the readers and their dramatic participation in its conclusion. As we saw in the tendency of the whole Gospel to look forward and back to the passion, so we see in the paradigmatic effect of the miracle stories the tendency of the silent conclusion to reaffirm the climactic confession of the centurion at the cross. At the same time that confession bears testimony to the truth of the narrator's introductory assertion that Jesus is the Christ, the Son of God, and to the reader's concluding insertion that the Son of God is the risen Lord. Because Mark suspended the narration at the crucial moment, the readers are extended the opportunity of speaking with the women the good news which this Gospel has anticipated since the first verse and of seeing with the disciples the reunion which is promised in the last verses.

Other Structures in the Gospel of Mark

The Transfiguration Narrative. The transfiguration of Jesus (Mark 9:2–9) might legitimately be classified as another miracle story. But its unique nature and frequent identification as a misplaced post-resurrection account, epiphany, or ascension story, demand separate treatment. Like the miracle stories, its structure is suggestive for the interpretation of 16:1–8.

Both accounts begin with a temporal note: the transfiguration took place "after six days"; the visit to the tomb "after three days." Three followers are in attendance on each occasion: Peter, James, and John on the first, Mary Magdalene, Mary, and Salome on the second. The white robe of the young man (angel) at the tomb reminds us of the glistening white garments of Jesus during the transfiguration. As with the empty tomb account, fear and silence follow the manifestation on the mountain: "For he [Peter] did not know what to say, for they were exceedingly afraid." A recognition statement comes from an other-worldly source in each story: in chapter nine a voice from heaven confirms that "this is my beloved son," while in 16:7 an angel (young man) identifies the risen Jesus. Both stories focus the function of sight on the person of Jesus. In 9:8 we read, "they no longer saw anyone with them, but Jesus only": 16:7 predicts "and there you will see him." A final command to silence in 9:9 matches the silence of the women in 16:8.

These structural similarities highlight the Marcan use of fear and silence. In line with our observations on miracle stories, we see

that silence is accompanied by speech and fear as a positive expression of worship. The disciples do not know what to say and yet
they speak, however haltingly. Their fear is not debilitating; because
it is motivated by the positive impulse of worship, they commence
acts of reverence, however irrelevant. The command to silence is not
absolute. The prohibition is temporary; the freedom to speak will
come with the event of the resurrection. Neither is their silence
complete; they discussed the incident and Jesus' cryptic reference to
a resurrection among themselves. The possible role of the transfiguration account as a post-resurrection narrative will be dealt with
in the next chapter. For now we can say that with the other miracle
stories, it prepares us to sense the structure and supply the features
of the concluding verses. When confronted with the supernatural
power and divine identity of Jesus, the women—like the disciples
when confronted with those impressions from the transfiguration—
reacted with a silence which gave birth to speech and a fear which
gave birth to action.

The Passion Narrative. Boomershine (1981a:237) points out patterning within the last three chapters of Mark. He sees in the stories
of Jesus' arrest, in the summaries of his trials, and in the resurrection
account, a four-fold pattern. In each major section comes 1) "the
fulfillment of an element of Jesus' passion-resurrection prophecies,"
2) "the establishment of norms of judgment in relation to right or
wrong responses," 3) "the appeal for identification with one of Jesus'
followers," and 4) "the narration of that follower's wrong response."
The suggestion of structural patterning is helpful; the assumption of
a negative conclusion is not necessarily borne out by another perspective on the passion narrative any more than it is by an analysis of
the miracle stories.

A. Farrer has pointed to interesting parallels in events before
and after Jesus' death (Kealy: 150).

a_1	Anointment by woman (14:3)	b_2	Body wrapped in cloth (15:46)
b_1	Offer of body as gift (14:8)	a_2	Women come to anoint (16:1)
c_1	Promise to go to Galilee (14:28)	e_2	Young man in white robe appears (16:5)
d_1	Disciples abandon Jesus (14:50)	c_2	"he is going before you to Galilee" (16:7)
e_1	Young man flees leaving robe (14:51–52)	d_2	"there you will see him" (16:7)

Some of these elements relate to the issue of foreshadowing which will be addressed in the next chapter. At this point it is enough to observe that the parallel structures suggest a set of reversals and confirmations. The young man moves from flight and silence in panel one to faithful presence and proclamation in panel two.[5] The fleeing disciples of the precrucifixion scene are still promised (by an authoritative angelic spokesman) that they will see Jesus in a re-union scene after the crucifixion and resurrection. Items a, b, and c are parallel confirmations which lead us to accept the correlation between d_1 and d_2 as well as between e_1 and e_2, i.e., to accept the possibility of the reversals.

Another pattern which emerges from the passion narrative is the frame created by the two anointing stories (14:3–9 and 16:1–8) (Perrin, 1977:29f). Commonalities—agents, references to burial, and emphasis on the disciples' lack of perception—are obvious. The significance of the first account for our study is its conclusion. The pericope closes with the words of Jesus, making reference to the facts that 1) the woman had anointed him for burying (14:8) and 2) "wherever the gospel is preached in the whole world, what she has done will be told in memory of her" (14:9). We suggest that the act of 14:8 is paradigmatic of the intended action of 16:1–8 and that the predicted effect of 14:9 is paradigmatic of the foreshadowed and prestructured though unnarrated effect of 16:1–8. In other words, just as the preanointing of 14:3 lends meaning and dramatic effect to the attempted anointing of 16:1, so the prediction of the publication of one woman's encounter suggests the publication of the incidents involving the three women. That the prediction of Jesus in 14:9 was fulfilled is supported by its very presence in the text; that the news entrusted to the women at the tomb was proclaimed as commanded by the angel is certified by the existence of the Gospel itself not to mention the existence of this closing pericope.

A final structural relationship within the passion narrative is the triad of references to women in 15:40–41, 15:42–47, and 16:1–8 (Perrin, 1977:14). These parallel panels yield the following details. In panel one, three women are the only followers near the cross; we are told that when Jesus was in Galilee they followed him and ministered to his needs. In panel two, only three women attend the

---

[5] Some question the identification of the young man of 14:51–52 with the one in 16:1–8. But whether or not the young man of each passage is the same, the two function paradigmatically as one.

burial of Jesus and observe the place of his interment. In panel three, three women are the first to return to the tomb; they are told of his resurrection and are commissioned to pass this news and instructions to meet Jesus on to his other followers. They leave in fear and silence.

The comparison of the panels of this triptych reveals a pattern of association and service. Panel one operates in two time frames. In the past of the story, when Jesus was in Galilee, the women followed him and ministered to him. In the story-present they stand near the cross, still following, companions with Jesus in death as in life. If they had failed they would have failed then, at the moment of the criminal's execution. In the second panel the women accompany the crucified Jesus to the tomb, observing the wrapping of his body and the sealing of the tomb; in summary, they saw where he was laid. If they had failed, they would have failed then, at the burial of this blasphemer and insurgent. In the third panel they are still following Jesus, going to his tomb, still ministering to Jesus, intending to anoint his body. If they had failed, they would have failed then, in the face of Roman guards and a weighty stone. The command in 16:7 to go and tell and the so-called failure of 16:8 must be seen in the light of this three-fold pattern of faithfulness and service.

Thus the paradigmatic effect of the miracle stories, the parallel patterning of the transfiguration account, and the literary structures of the passion narrative accomplish three ends. They place the functions of fear and silence in a basically positive light; they imply a proclamation which is actualized outside of the text but in the story by the participation of the reader; and they foreshadow the fulfillment of the angelic mandate in 16:7. It remains to be seen how conclusively a study of suggestive foreshadowing and an analysis of the synecdochal function of the ending confirm this judgment.

Chapter VII

"A FOREGONE CONCLUSION": SUSPENSION AND SIGNIFICANCE IN THE ENDING OF MARK

"Welcome to all we have snatched like this
From doubt, the mouths re-endowed with power
Of speech, after knowing what silence is."

—RILKE[1]

"We can know more than we can tell."

—POLANYI (1967:4)

The insights of modern literary theory have given us eyes for openness and minds for the meaning-effect of that openness in all literature. We are now better prepared to follow other New Testament interpreters in arguing for coherent closure at Mark 16:8 and to gauge the effect such an ending would have on its readers. The examples of openness and suspended endings from ancient literature have confirmed that the use of that device is not a modern phenomenon. They have also demonstrated the means by which authors are able to make provision for an absent ending. In each case the writers employed one or more of a trio of techniques. The structure of a work, its beginning and emplotted middle, causes the reader to assume a certain shape for the conclusion; even when that ending is not realized in the text, the readers sense the intended ending from the assumed shape of the absent ending. Foreshadowing, allusions to incidents in the future of the story, is a second common means of preparing readers for an ending and of providing the raw materials for the mental construction of an ending omitted from the text. On occasion a third device is used—the synecdochal

---

[1] This passage and others which demonstrate Rilke's appreciation of silence can be found in *Sonnets to Orpheus* (Purchase Press, 1981).

function of one narrative item to represent the larger unnarrated conclusion.

A close reading of the Gospel of Mark suggests the kind of openness common to modern literature but characteristic of much great ancient literature as well—a sense of closure achieved in spite of and by means of the suspension of the narrative climax from the text. A careful analysis of Mark also reveals the same techniques employed by other literary works to achieve that sense of an ending. Petersen's analysis (1980:163) has pointed to their presence. "But the irony of 16:8, combined with the implicit directions provided by the plotting of expectations and satisfactions, constitutes an artful substitute for the obvious." His reference to "plotting" suggests the effect of the structural shape of the whole on the interpretation of the ending. The "expectations and satisfactions" parallel what we have described as foreshadowing in other texts. And his delightful phrase, "an artful substitute for the obvious," is precisely what we observed in the synecdochal substitution of the ending which is there for the ending which is not there.

The previous chapter explored the structural framework of Mark and the influence of that structure on our reading of the ending of Mark. This chapter completes our survey of the three chief techniques by describing the use and effect of foreshadowing and the synecdochal function of the empty tomb account. The chapter closes with an interpretation and an analysis of the effect of the suspended ending on readers of the Gospel.

Suggestive Foreshadowing in the Gospel of Mark

Duckworth's work (1966:37) on foreshadowing in Homer has demonstrated that an ancient writer often "strives to increase the reader's interest not in spite of the readers' foreknowledge, but by means of it." By developing a sense of suspense, by imposing a retarding influence on the flow of the plot, or by the use of repeated prophecies, the author supplies the readers with the appropriate mood, opportunity, and materials for understanding the intent of the conclusion. Similar procedures are used, knowingly or not, by the author of Mark.

Some might argue again at this point that such careful foreshadowing is outside the ability or interest of Mark. But Mark has obviously used a sophisticated method of "back-shadowing," the process of introducing various characters or events from the past into the plot by means of allusion or quotation. Abraham, Moses, David,

Elijah, and Isaiah are read intelligently into the "story-past" on only the slightest allusion from the text. With no introduction whatsoever, John the Baptist, Herod, and Pilate are ushered on-stage by the narrator; and yet readers easily find a place for them in the coherent if unnarrated background of the Gospel account. Thus, "if the gospel contains allusions so delicate and recondite to earlier and incited texts, why should there not be internal allusions and dependencies of equal subtlety?" (Kermode, 1979:60). In other words, if "the earlier events are . . . folded into the plotted segment of time through allusions or quotations," there is no reason why subsequent unnarrated events could not have been "folded into it through predictions whose fulfillment he does not emplot" (Petersen: 157).

This process of foreshadowing and foreshadowing climactic events which are assumed but which never surface in the text is nothing more than what many readers have sensed all along. Hunter (1965:149) hypothesized that the original ending of Mark was lost; but he sensed that "we have enough to show us what the sequel to the Crucifixion was." The ending was sufficiently foreshadowed so that the suspension of its narration did not interfere with the readerly comprehension of it. F. C. Grant (1951:916), on the other hand, accepts 16:8 as the original ending; but he too sensed the foreshadowed conclusion. "Thus the Gospel of Mark closes without an account of the Resurrection, or of any appearances of the risen Jesus, but it everywhere presupposes the resurrection of our Lord."

Mark includes a number of significant prophecies which are not fulfilled in the text. In Mark 13 Jesus predicts the desecration and destruction of the Temple, the coming of international warfare, and the occurrence of cosmic calamities. The disciples have no doubt that these events will occur; their only question is "when?" The readers of Mark are presented with these same prophecies from the mouth of Jesus, predictions of future events, predictions "which carry the evangelist's total 'story' beyond his actual 'plotted narrative'" (Wilder: 296–299). The words of Jesus foreshadow events which for the reader occur in the story-future even though they are never narrated in the text. Like the disciples, the readers have come to accept the trustworthiness of Jesus' words.

More to the point are the passages which foreshadow the events seemingly omitted from the ending of Mark. The resurrection itself, the post-resurrection appearances, and future faithful proclamation by the disciples are all, in the literal sense of the phrase, foregone conclusions, on the basis of foreshadowing. These suggestive passages are concentrated in the passion prediction units; in the instructional sections of chapters 10, 13, and 14; and in the Transfiguration account. Of course, the whole Gospel from first to last presupposes a resurrection. The good news of which Mark speaks in his title makes sense only in the context of an ultimate reversal of the crucifixion. The last verses (16:6–7) reiterate a conclusion which has been foreshadowed throughout.

Predictions of Jesus' passion come from his own lips in 8:31, 9:31, and 10:33–34. In each case pointed reference is made to his suffering, his death, and his resurrection: "after three days he will rise (again)." This trio of references to the triad of events begins at the turning point of the Gospel, Peter's profession that Jesus is the Christ (8:29), and recurs at regular and significant geographical intervals as Jesus' band moves from Caesarea Philippi through Galilee and into Judea where the final confrontation will occur. The straightforwardness and significance of the predictions cannot be ignored; these passages form the core of reader expectation in the latter half of the book. Thus the event of the resurrection is clearly foreshadowed.

Perrin (1977:20f) makes much of the fact that misunderstanding by the disciples and corrective teaching by Jesus follow each prediction. It is also helpful to note the elements which precede each prediction. Just before the first passion prediction (8:31), Peter responds to Jesus' question with an affirmation of his identity. Jesus counsels silence in the matter: "tell no one." Immediately preceding the second passion prediction (9:31) Mark narrates Jesus' movement toward Jerusalem and notes that he prevented the publication of his whereabouts: "he would not have any one know it." Evidently the disciples were prone to announce Jesus' arrival and explain his identity in the towns along their route. In the third instance, just before the final prediction of the crucifixion and resurrection (10:33–34), Mark notes their movement toward Jerusalem, mentions Jesus' leadership, and points out the willingness of the disciples to follow even in the midst of their mounting fear and amazement: "And they were on the road, going up to Jerusalem, and Jesus was walking ahead of them; and they were amazed, and those who followed were afraid."

The context of these prediction units reveals that they are associated with 1) proclamation or attempted proclamation of Jesus' identity; 2) silence regarding Jesus and commanded by Jesus; and 3) fear which is occasioned by (and does not hinder) following Jesus to the place of confrontation. Just as the clear predictions of Jesus' death and resurrection prepare the readers for those events and provide them with a basis for sensing the ending which is not fully narrated, so the setting of the prediction units prepares the readers to expect proclamation, silence, and fear in the context of the resurrection. These are precisely the elements in 16:1–8 which attend the sensed but absent narratives of the resurrection and post-resurrection appearances.

The corrective teaching which follows the three predictions of death and resurrection focuses on the nature of discipleship in the light of the prophesied events. Following the prediction in chapter 8, Jesus emphasizes self-denial and continued following not just in spite of but in the light of the cross. Subsequent to 9:31 is the teaching about humility and childlikeness as the basis of true greatness. The discussion with James and John about greatness and servanthood in Jesus' kingdom succeeds the third prediction. In each case Jesus' assumption that the disciples will follow him even after the death and resurrection and that they need instructions for that difficult time leads the readers to expect just such an outcome. Thus the three prediction units foreshadow the event of the resurrection, a crisis of proclamation and silence, a response of fear, and continued discipleship.

Among the many prophecies in the instructional scenes of chapter 10, the apocalyptic section of chapter 13, and the hortatory passages in chapter 14 are predictions directly applicable to the behavior of the disciples after the resurrection. The disciples will receive a hundredfold what they have given up for the cause of following Jesus (10:30). James and John will "drink his cup," i.e. die a martyr's death for the sake of the gospel (10:39). Peter, James, John, and Andrew will be arrested and beaten because of their affiliation with Jesus; but their hearing before government officials will give them the opportunity to preach the gospel (13:9–11). This last passage foreshadows not only severe persecution but the accomplishment of an international proclamation of the gospel, the good news about Jesus. The worldwide proclamation of the gospel by these disciples is also predicted by Jesus in 14:9. "All these prophecies affirm that the disciples will continue to follow Jesus and will suffer in the course of their proclaiming his good news of the rule of God" (Rhoads and Michie: 97). And besides assuring the reader of the disciples' role in proclamation after the resurrection, Jesus' own words foreshadow another related event, their reunion with Jesus in

Galilee: "But after I am raised up, I will go before you to Galilee" (14:28).

The fulfillment of these predictions is assured to the readers not only by virtue of the general confidence they have in the trust-worthiness of the prophet and the reliability of the narrator but also because of "the prophecies about the disciples which come to fulfill-ment within the narrative" (Rhoads and Michie: 96). Jesus tells Simon and Andrew he will make them fishers of men, and he does (1:16–18). Jesus tells two disciples they will find a colt for his entrance into Jerusalem, and they do (11:1–6). Jesus tells them they will find a room readied for the Passover, and they do (14:13–16). Some predictions regarding the disciples are fulfilled in the text; the readers expect the fulfillment of those which are never narrated but are clearly foreshadowed in the text, namely their reunion with Jesus in Galilee and their proclamation of the gospel after the resurrection.

The third concentration of foreshadowing relating to the resur-rection is Mark's account of the transfiguration. The fifth chapter of this study has already explored the structural potential of that ac-count for anticipating the unfinished shape of 16:1–8; a brief second glance from a thematic perspective is in order. The pericope (9:2–9) has all the marks of an epiphany—the mountain setting, the glisten-ing garments, supernatural manifestations, and a heavenly voice. Many commentators argue that it is in fact a post-resurrection epiphany, the description of a reappearance which Mark has acci-dentally or deliberately placed at the center of the plot rather than at its conclusion.

Whether or not it is a post-resurrection scene misplaced from its proper position in the story, the transfiguration stands as a pre-resurrection account in the text. One effect is to focus the readers' attention on the incipient resurrection long before it actually occurs in the story and thereby enhance the anticipation of it. A second effect is to make possible the omission of a post-resurrection ap-pearance account from the conclusion of the text while supplying the readers with the assurance of its occurrence and an understand-ing of the nature of the experience for the disciples. Trompf (1972:319) argued that an account of the resurrection is demanded in the Gospel because of the narration of the transfiguration event, that is, that Mark's Gospel must have originally ended with a post-resurrection appearance clearly narrated in the text. Our research leads us to accept his logic but not his conclusion: the transfiguration foreshadows the post-resurrection reappearance of Jesus so graphically that the readers supply in their minds what is omitted in the text. Fuller (1980:67) claims even more for the anticipatory effect of the transfiguration narrative:

> In the light of Mark 9:9, Mark 16:7 points forward not only to the appearances to the disciples (and especially to Peter) but also to the publication of the messianic secret and the inauguration of the mission. Mark thus achieves in a highly oblique manner what the later Evangelists achieve more directly through the missionary charges which they put into the mouth of the Risen One.

The "highly oblique manner" of foreshadowing to which Fuller refers is complemented by the somewhat less oblique foreshadowing by which the passion predictions create anticipation for the resurrection and subsequent events. Oblique or not, suggestive foreshadowing within the Gospel points clearly to the details as well as the shape of the suspended ending which the readers must create in its absence from the text. The readers expect and in their expectation read a risen Jesus, appearing and present to his disciples, inaugurating a ministry of missionary proclamation among his fearful followers.

The Synecdochal Function of the Ending of Mark

Frank Kermode (1979:65) has enunciated the literary principle on the basis of which we read the muted if not truncated endings of the *Iliad* and other ancient texts: he insists

> that we can derive the sense of fulfilled expectation, of satisfactory closure, from texts that actually do not provide what we ask, but give us instead something that, out of pure desire for completion, we are prepared to regard as a metaphor or a synecdoche for the ending that is not there.

Several facets of this statement are noteworthy. Some texts do not end the way we expect. But they have told us what to expect. What they do give us—the way they do end—in some way fulfills our expectations of the ending and provides a sense of satisfactory closure. The involvement of the reader together with the author makes this outcome possible, since the author's device depends on the ability of the reader to follow the story and the desire of the reader to finish the story. A general term to describe the relationship between present and absent elements of the ending might be metaphor; but the relationship is not simply that of implied comparison. Perhaps a less general term would be metonymy, the use of one word to suggest another, as when a sign or an attribute of a thing stands for the thing itself. But Kermode uses the specific designation synecdoche, a device in which one thing (the part, the whole, the species, or the genus) stands for another (the whole, the part, the genus, or the species, respectively). Whether we choose metonymy or synecdoche, the relationship described comes very close to defining what we perceive to be the integral connection between the elements of the ending which is there and those of the ending which is not there in the Gospel of Mark.

The empty tomb account has been seen by some as an ending whose meaning is absence, a reversal of expectations created throughout the Gospel for resurrection and reunion (Crossan, 1978:41–55). For others the empty tomb story is the introduction to accounts of the reappearance of the risen Jesus which have been lost from the text. But the empty tomb account may well be the intended ending of the text and may function as a synecdoche for the suspended ending of the story. The *Iliad* also ended with a burial; but the burial of Hector signified far more than the passing of one Trojan hero. It conveyed the conclusions of the larger story, a part implying the whole, a burial signifying the death of one people and the victory of another. The empty tomb, signifying both the death and resurrection of Jesus, stands for and ties together these events, the one narrated, the other unnarrated. As Marin (1976:35–36) puts it, in the parallel terminology of structuralism, "The absence of the dead body in the sepulchre is the significant of the resurrection." The empty tomb is the dramatic scene with which Mark chooses to close his Gospel—dramatic not so much because it omits the resurrection and post-resurrection accounts but because it suggests them, demands them, in the minds of the readers. As such it is an open ending which provides coherent closure and it is a literary absence which suggests an actual presence.

Although it has a synecdochal function and a significance all its own, the empty tomb is not presented by Mark as the evidence for the resurrection event. The words of revelation by the young man (angel), not an open and empty sepulchre, elicit the fear and drive the women to stunned silence (Lane: 588–589). These words found in 16:6–7 follow the pattern of the report of the angelos, the herald of Greek drama. In play after play (see chapter III) we found the climactic scene communicated not by action but by the words of either one of the participants or an eyewitness observer. Account replaces and stands for action; the announcement is the synecdoche which signifies the incident. Trompf (1972: 322) recognized this phenomenon as one of the features which sets Mark apart from the other gospels: 16:1–8 lacks the "divine actions of Jesus." But this lack is not absolute or final, and neither is it to be overcome by the addition of the "original ending." The passage is a satisfactory ending because its focus, the proclamation of the angel, stands in for the events it mentions.

These verses offer *in discourse* the resurrection of Jesus ("he has risen"), the repetition of the good news by the women ("go, tell his disciples"), and the reappearance and reunion of Jesus with his followers ("there you will see him"). Fuller (1980:53) points out the connection of 16:6–7 with the resurrection and the reappearance.

> The function of the angelophany is to announce the resurrection. As such, it plays a vital role in the passion narrative, for that narrative must end not with the death of Jesus, but with the resurrection. . . . The angelophany, asserting as it does that the resurrection was made known by revelation, was a natural device for achieving that end.

Petersen (1980: 154–155) agrees that the prediction of the resurrection is fulfilled in "he has risen"; but he argues that the prediction of a meeting in Galilee is not fulfilled because of the women's silence in verse 8. I would suggest that the authoritative report of the angel explains the absence of Jesus from the tomb *and* the absence of a direct narration of the events of Jesus' resurrection and reappearance to his followers. The presence of the discourse about the risen Jesus ("he has risen") overcomes the absence of the crucified and entombed Jesus by raising and making him present in the readers' minds. I would likewise argue that the angelic proclamation explains the fear of the women and the absence of any narration about their announcement to the disciples. The presence of the discourse about the women ("go, tell his disciples and Peter that he is going before you in Galilee; there you will see him") overcomes the absence of their words and the absence of any narration about their report by speaking their words for them in the readers' minds.

Such an interpretation is not only natural (to recall Fuller's term) but likely on the grounds of historical precedent and practical observation. We have already noted how Biblical as well as classical texts close with reported discourse in the place of narrated action. But practically speaking, how do we read 16:6–7? One modern scholar (Smith: 371–372) admits,

> Even if there had been a narrative centered on Peter [a post-resurrection narrative] we should have been shown no more than is already implied in the affirmation that . . . Jesus was the Son of God . . . that he is risen . . . and that his presence is to be found in Galilee. . . .

In other words, the report provides us with all the information we need about succeeding events and makes their suspension from the text not only possible but more powerful. Evidently ancient readers made the same move from discourse to deed. Some early texts transcribe the report of the angel as if Jesus himself were present, appearing to the women and instructing them. Codex Bezae (Cantabrigiensis, D) and the old Latin Codex Bobiensis (k) contain the variant "I am going before you to Galilee, there you will see me, even as I told you." Two aspects of this alteration are noteworthy. First is the recognition that the words of the angel are representative of the divine words of Jesus which in turn are representative of the divine actions of Jesus. Second is the ease with which an appearance by Jesus is read into the announcement of an appearance by Jesus. Words are synecdoches for actions and prophecies for their fulfillments.

Petersen (1980:156) raises the problem which 16:8 creates for this interpretation of 16:6–7 but appears to answer his own hesitations by pointing toward the synecdochal function of that verse: "16:8 is either an intentional reversal of expectations or an ironic substitute of the obvious continuation of events implied by the narrator." Petersen clearly chooses the second possibility. This analysis is almost exactly what I intend by my use of the word synecdoche and this application of the concept is the logical outcome of my understanding of the structural function of fear and silence in Marcan miracle stories (see chapter VI). Fear and silence are emphasized in the text; but they signify what the doctrine of good continuance demands—faith, following, and proclamation. So, like the account of the empty tomb which stands for the suspended account of the resurrection and like the words of the angel which stand for the suspended accounts of reporting, reappearing, and reuniting, the account of amazement, flight, and silence in 16:8 suggests an event (the resurrection) for their awe-struck minds to fear, a path (the journey to the abode of the disciples) for their stumbling feet to follow, and a message (the news of the resurrection and the command to gather) for their stammering lips to dare to repeat.

Interestingly enough, the three synecdochal elements we have identified—the empty tomb, the angelic announcement, and the women's reaction—all look both backward into the text and forward into the story-future. The tomb signifies the death of Jesus which Mark has described in some detail; the emptiness suggests a resurrection which is not described. The angelic announcement refers to Jesus' own past prophecies ("there you will see him as he told you"); it also foreshadows Jesus' own future actions, his progress to Galilee and gathering with his disciples. The reaction of the women (16:8) "redirects the reader's attention back to the immediately preceding words of the young man . . ." (Petersen: 162); but those words also drive the readers ahead past the fear, past the silence, to the fulfillment of the angel's words and the satisfaction of the readers' expectations for a post-resurrection appearance and meeting with Jesus. In this way the elements of 16:1–8, anchored as they are in the text, in the story-past, function metonymically or synecdochally to suggest elements of the story-future which Mark has suspended from his text.[2]

Summary and Interpretation

We introduced this study by noting "the dignity and restraint of the narrative [16:1–8], the absence of any attempt to describe the resurrection itself or to depict an appearance of the Risen Christ, features which stand out in relief when the narrative is compared with later accounts in the Gospels and the Gospel of Peter" (Taylor: 603). The introduction also explored modern literary theories related to openendedness and the meaning-effect of suspended endings. Succeeding chapters described the presence and significance of this phenomenon in Greco-Roman and Biblical literature, works more contemporary with the Gospel of Mark. This and the previous

---

[2] One other possible synecdochal relationship is that of the whole Gospel standing for one of its absent parts, the resurrection/report/reunion sequence we have been discussing. The very existence of the document testifies to the fulfillment of the women's assignment to report the news, to the acceptance of that report and obedience by the disciples, and to a faith based on the resurrection announcement. "A material proof of their ultimate belief . . . is the existence of this written account, which portrays Jesus as the Christ, the Son of God" (Smith: 371).

chapter have demonstrated the devices by which Mark communicated his conclusion without narrating it—devices common to ancient literature. We draw our study to a close with a final comment on the suspended ending of Mark and its meaning.

As in all literary works there are minor omissions throughout the Gospel and in the closing verses. We are not told, for instance, who rolled the stone from the doorway (a major concern of the women) or that the tomb was in fact empty (a major concern of interpreters). But these are examples of unessential or obvious details to be filled in or not by the imagination of the readers. More crucially, the final scene omits a description of the resurrection itself while supplying the setting for and immediate aftermath of the event. There is a burial and a visit to the tomb for embalming; there is an open tomb and a messenger with news of an empty tomb. But Mark, like the other canonical Gospels, refuses to describe the central action. Other writers sensed and supplemented the gap Mark leaves. A gloss between 16:3 and 16:4 in Codex Bobiensis (k) adds: "suddenly at the third hour of the day, there was darkness over the whole earth, and angels descended from heaven, and rising in the splendor of the living God they ascended together with him, and immediately it was light" (Lane: 582). But this account too offers only surrounding circumstances and does not attempt a description of the actual raising.

The Gospel of Peter, a second century apocryphal gospel, includes one of the few straighforward attempts at a description of the resurrection.

> 34. The morning of the Sabbath dawned; a crowd came from Jerusalem and its surroundings in order that they might see the tomb sealed up. 35. In the night before the dawn of the Lord's day, while the soldiers guarded two by two, there was a great noise in heaven, 36. and they saw the heavens open and two men, having great splendor, come down from there and draw near the tomb. 37. The stone which had been placed at the door rolled away by itself and moved to the side. The tomb was opened and the two youths went in. 38. When the soldiers saw this, they awakened the centurion and the elders, for they were there on guard. 39. As they recounted what they had seen, again they saw three men coming out of the tomb; two supported one of them and a cross followed them. 40. The heads of the two reached to heaven, but the one whom they bore with their hands reached beyond the heavens. 41. And they

heard a voice speaking from the heavens, "Have you preached to those who are sleeping?" 42. And obediently, (a voice) was heard from the cross, "Yes" (Cartlidge and Dungan: 85).

This example is obviously out of character with the tone and approach of Mark and the other canonical Gospels (see verse 40); but the attempt is instructive. That some author attempted to fill in the gap demonstrates that 1) readers sensed that something was indeed missing when the resurrection event was not narrated, and 2) readers sensed what was missing—a resurrection—even if their depiction of it was highly fanciful. Readers sensed the presence of the event of the resurrection in spite of the absence of its description.

The most dramatic omissions in Mark's conclusion are the totally excluded events of the return and report of the women to the disciples, the reappearance of Jesus, and his reunion with his disciples. An interpretation which focuses narrowly and exclusively on the text of 16:1–8 sees only the absence of an appropriate ending, the absence of Jesus, and the absence of post-resurrection report and reunion. But an interpretation which takes into account the common literary devices at Mark's disposal and the meaning-potential of a suspended ending makes sense where others see only absence. On this basis we can make three assertions. First, Mark 16:1–8, in spite of its openness and omissions, achieves satisfactory closure. This opinion is not a modern theoretical imposition on an ancient text; it is an opinion based on careful comparison with the endings of other ancient literary types. Like the *Iliad* which ends "so precipitately on this high note of tension" (Walsh), like the *Aeneid* which ends "in a minor key, and on a falling cadence" (Sayers: 26), like the typical epic which "though it must have a close, does not have an end" and closes "in such a way as to leave us with a vivid sense of going-on" (Duckworth: 28), Mark achieves "bona fide narrative closure" (Petersen: 159) in its very openness. The closing verses have proven to be what Farrer (1951:174) claimed of them, "a strong, complex refrain, answering all the ends of previous sections in the Gospel to which we might expect it to answer." They achieve a consonance which balances the discontinuity created by an abrupt beginning and meet, in narrative or in suspended narrative, all our expectations for fulfillment. Mark 16:6–7 "directs the reader's imagination to provide the proper closure to the narrator's story" (Petersen: 163); but it is the omissions, the suspensions, the seeming lack of closure which allows the reader the freedom to perform that task.

Second, Mark 16:1–8 affirms the resurrection of Jesus in spite of Mark's failure to describe the event itself or any post-resurrection appearances. The structure of Marcan miracle stories leads us to expect a factum at the heart of such an account; foreshadowing makes the resurrection an indispensable component of the gospel story; and the words of the angel are an effective substitute for the description of the events. These conclusions confirm the opinions of Lightfoot (1938:58), who wrote that "to the fact of the resurrection St. Mark has given full expression in 16:1–8." These insights also counsel caution in adopting the appealing suggestions of many modern critics who see the parousia or an ascension/parousia construct as the focus of Mark's conclusion rather than the resurrection. The Jesus whom the angel predicts they will see is the one Jesus himself foreshadowed they would see, the risen as well as the returning Lord. The paradigmatic structure of Mark's stories indicates that the fear of the women is not the fear of an unknown future, a parousia which lies before them, but the fear of a seen and known (if not fully understood) phenomenon which they have observed. Far from forcing the readers into a new complex of events surrounding the ascension and parousia, the closing words of the angel push the readers back into the past, to reconsider the crucifixion ("who was crucified"), the burial ("where they laid him"), and the resurrection ("he has risen"). Rather than demand a substitution of parousia for resurrection, the strange silence of the women and the narrator in verse 8 direct the reader to the events which have just transpired and the divine words which have just interpreted them—the demonstration of supernatural power in the resurrection and the angelic testimony to it.

The omission of post-resurrection appearances from Mark has led some scholars to another assertion—that one of Mark's chief points is the absence of Jesus from the experience of his followers until the parousia. This interpretation reaches a climax in Crossan's insightful "theology of absence." Without disagreeing with the reality of the experience—then or now—of living in the absence of the immediate presence of the risen Christ, we must say that this does not appear to be the main emphasis of Mark's conclusion. There is considerable evidence that the absence is literary and that the effect of a literary absence is not so much the creation of a sense of existential abandonment as it is the creation of a sense of powerful presence. Crossan (1978:53) himself suggests this possibility: "It is also worth noting that absence is itself a most paradoxical category. . . . Indeed it may well be but the deepest most permanent form of presence." What Crossan means psychologically of the experience of Jesus' followers is true literarily of the experience of Mark's "followers," his readers: the suspension of the narration of a post-resurrection appearance makes the impact of that foreshadowed event even greater in the expectant minds of the readers who have followed Jesus in the story. Absence from the text is not necessarily absence from the story; the absence of the narration of an event does not necessarily remove and may in fact create the sense of that event.

Third, Mark 16:1–8 assumes the obedience of the women and the other disciples to the instructions of the angel—that is, it assumes report and reunion—in spite of Mark's failure to narrate the enactment of that obedience. Foreshadowing, structural patterns, and the synecdochal function of 16:6–7 all lead us to expect proclamation and renewed following. We must read 16:8 literarily in the light of the dynamics of the whole Gospel and its immediate context rather than read the whole Gospel and 16:1–8 in the light of a literal interpretation of 16:8. That literary reading—one based on an appreciation for common literary techniques—sheds a different light on what is seen by many commentators as a negative conclusion with failure as its theme and unfinished in its form.

> That the women are described as saying nothing to anybody . . . clearly does not mean that they did not tell their experience to their close friends. It probably means no more than that they were too terrified and in too much of a hurry to stop and speak to anybody they chanced to meet between the tomb and wherever they were staying (Moule, 1965:133).

If this is true, then the silence of 16:8 is a "stupid" silence (Kermode) only in the etymological sense of benumbed or astonished.

Therefore, not only in spite of the fear and silence but in a sense in the light of the fear and silence, an awareness of the literary potential of the suspended ending allows us to sense the scenario of the omitted scenes. The women pass on the confirming and guiding words of the angel. The disciples follow their instructions and are reunited with Jesus. They are renewed in their relationship and recommissioned for ministry. Although Perrin (1977:31) insists that the absence of a post-resurrection appearance removes the possibility of "restitution and renewal of trust," everything about 16:7 "suggests the possibility of restoration" (Rhoads and Michie: 97). Peter (the familiar and affectionate nickname once again) is personally addressed, Jesus is still going ahead of them, they are still welcome and expected to follow, the site for the new start is Galilee where their life and ministry together had begun, and there they will see Jesus. Mark does not narrate these events, but the fact that he puts them so precisely in the mouth of one of his characters, his herald, demonstrates that he could have narrated them. Instead, he supplies "the satisfaction of the expectation generated in the prediction of a meeting between Jesus and the eleven in Galilee" (Petersen: 163). We read faithful following rather than failure.

So it is that Crossan's paradox—absence as the most permanent form of presence—is precisely the point. Literary absences do not necessarily produce theological absences. We do not assume that since the risen Jesus is not present in the text of Mark that he was not present in the post-resurrection experience of his followers. We do not assume that since the women file no report and the disciples do not follow Jesus to a Galilean reunion in the text of Mark that Mark's story does not imply and include those events. But what kind of presence do these absences produce and by what means? The rest of the story, motivated by the text but molded as it is told by the readers, is the middle term which mediates between the absence in the literary text and any theological presence. The presence of the risen Jesus is not to be found textually, solely in the words of the last lines of a work we call the Gospel of Mark. Neither is he to be found existentially, solely in the pious or ecstatic experience of believers. The risen Jesus is to be found in the story which takes shape in the minds of Mark's readers, as his text draws to a close. Jesus is present in and for the future, to be sure; the parousia emphasis is not without merit. And Jesus is present in the past, insofar as story depends on testimony and testimony on event; the perspective of history is not illegitimate. But Jesus is also and perhaps most directly present in the readers' present, as they tell the absent ending of his story.

This relationship between the Lord who is absent from the text and the Lord who is present in the story reminds us of the roots of the technique of the suspended ending in theories of reader response. The specific demands which are placed on a reader who must fill in an absent ending are an important aspect of our literary analysis of the meaning of 16:1–8. Our goal throughout this study has been to ask how an intelligent and interested reader would have understood Mark's conclusion. Our interpretive summary of 16:1–8 has instinctively and deliberately mentioned the involvement of the reader at a number of points. If we have ignored some of the recent contributions to the analysis of 16:1–8, like the interesting redaction-critical separation of 16:8a and 16:8b (Weeden, 1971:47–48), it is because some of the modern approaches on which those conclusions are based ignore the dynamics of reading. They fail to take into account the question we have kept as foremost: how would a first-time reader of Codex Vaticanus have understood those closing verses? Even though the author of Mark has prepared his readers to make sense of the abrupt ending, he has not completely prepared them for the abruptness itself. It would still have come as a surprise, still have created suspense, still have called forth reactions different from those elicited by a fully narrated conclusion. The reactions are two-fold: what the reader would have done to the ending and what the ending would have done to the reader.

The suspended ending causes the reader to act on the ending. Our contention has been that readers would have been forced to fill in the suspended ending. With a background of interest in Jesus and of instruction regarding his resurrection and subsequent appearances, most readers knew the general contents of the omitted scenes and supplied an ending appropriate to their faith or general knowledge. After having read the Gospel of Mark up to the point of this conclusion, these same readers had been provided with predictions and paradigmatic patterns which confirmed those traditional contents but in its own special way gave a unique shape—Mark's shape—to those unnarrated events. What is there in the foreshortened ending generated its own clear clues about the ending they must sense in the absence of a full narration. But this reaction, the desire and the ability to fill in the absent ending brought about another reaction.

Just as the suspended ending causes the reader to act on the ending, so it works in a special way to cause the reader to be affected by that ending. One response readers make to all literature, suspension aside, is identification with certain characters; this applies to Mark's Gospel as well. Some readers might identify with Jesus and reject the disciples (Tolbert); others might identify with Jesus but maintain a sympathetic interest in the disciples (Dewey); and still others would identify with the disciples and then reject them when they reject Jesus (Tannehill). But talk of rejection is too extreme for the relation of the characters in the story and the readers of the story; the matter of identification is too complex for such simple, straight-forward solutions. The suspended ending causes a complex impact on readers which runs deeper than simple rejection or acceptance and reaches beyond the simple process of identifying with this or that character.

As the ancient rhetorician Demetrius (*On Style*, 119–120) taught, "some things seem to be more significant when not expressed" and those omissions "will make an expression more forcible." So it is with the ending of Mark, "a highly dramatic climax, whose very abruptness and mysterious refusal to say more stimulate the imagination" (Moule, 1965:132–133). By narrating only the reactions of the first audience—the fear and silence of the women—and not the events to which they were reacting or the outcome of their reactions, the author "also seeks to provoke the hearer or reader of the story in the present to react" (Theissen: 167). But this stimulation, this provocation, must have some focus and take some form.

One suggestion is that the purpose of the dramatic device of suspension is to allow readers to see themselves as the chosen, those who see Jesus, the revelation of the secret of God, even when all others including the disciples are blinded to the truth.[3] Apart from the negative assessment of the response of the disciples implied by this view, it may be correct in suggesting that readers would have a sense of their own clear insight, heightened by the absence of a clearly stated comprehension by the disciples. But the readers have never really been in the dark. The title of the Gospel gave away the secret even before it informed the readers that there was a secret. The primary effect of the suspended ending on the readers does include a sense of understanding but not necessarily of superior understanding; and that sense is not so much the privilege of being chosen as it is the opportunity to choose.

Whether the women reported the news and the disciples gathered with Jesus to become eyewitnesses of the resurrection (as I think Mark implies) or not, the fact that their response is unnarrated concretizes the options available to those who have been told that Jesus arose from the dead. The options include appropriate action,

---

[3] This tack is taken by H. J. Ebeling in *The Messianic Secret and the Message of the Evangelist Mark*.

inappropriate action, and inaction; proclamation, indiscriminate communication, and a total lack of communication; and obedient following, passive acceptance, and rejection. The suspension creates the necessity of choosing among these various options, of providing a resolution to the story in the experience of the reader rather than in the text. The emphasis of the Gospel thus shifts from past history to present proclamation, from chronicle to commission, largely on the strength of that sense of exclusion (Fuller: 68). It creates a sense of obedience in the reader which would have been easier to avoid had Mark narrated a conclusion.

This existential crisis of following is inherently connected at the point of the suspended ending with the literary crisis of followability. Because we read in the ending the beginning, we are forced to look back for the shape of the ending. Because we read the ending as a new beginning, we are forced to look forward for the substance of the ending. "While the narrator may be finished, the reader's work begins; for the women's reaction becomes the prism through which the entire preceding narrative must be reviewed" (Petersen: 159). The ending initiates the process of retrospection and of expectation; it demands that we ask—because it did not tell—"what has happened?" and "what will happen?" in Mark's story and in the reader's story. The suspended ending of the Gospel of Mark, the absence which he forces us to sense and of which he prepares us to make sense, is a significant factor in the merging of those stories.

BIBLIOGRAPHY

Achilles Tatius
1917   *The Adventures of Leucippe and Cleitophon*. London: William Heinemann.

Achtemeier, Paul J.
1975   *Mark*. Philadelphia: Fortress.

Alter, Robert
1981   *The Art of Biblical Narrative*. New York: Basic.

Aristotle
1952   *Poetics*, in *The Works of Aristotle*, Vol. II. Chicago: Encyclopedia Britannica.

Auerbach, Erich
1953   *Mimesis*. Princeton: Princeton University.

Austin, Norman
1978   "The Function of Digressions in the Iliad," in John Wright, ed., *Essays on the Iliad*. Bloomington: Indiana University.

Barclay, William
1975   *Introduction to the First Three Gospels*. Philadelphia: Westminster.

Bernstein, Leonard
1976   *The Unanswered Question: Six Talks at Harvard*. Cambridge: Harvard University.

Betz, H. D.
1978   "Early Christian Miracles," in Robert Detweiler, ed., *Semeia* 4. Missoula: Scholars.

Beye, C. R.
1972   *The Iliad, Odyssey and Epic Tradition*. Gloucester, Massachusetts: Peter Smith.

Bleich, David
1981   *Subjective Criticism*. Baltimore: Johns Hopkins.

Boomershine, Thomas E., and Bartholomew, Gilbert L.

1981a "Mark 16:8 and the Apostolic Commission," *Journal of Biblical Literature* 100 (June): 225–239.

1981b "The Narrative Technique of Mark 16:8." *Journal of Biblical Literature* 100 (June): 213–223.

Booth, Wayne
1961 *The Rhetoric of Fiction*. Chicago: University of Chicago.

Bowen, Elizabeth
1958 "Rx for a Story Worth Telling." *New York Times Book Review* (August).

Bowman, John
1965 *The Gospel of Mark: The New Christian Jewish Passover Haggadah*. Leiden: E. J. Brill.

Branscomb, Harvie
The Gospel of Mark. New York: Harper and Brothers.

Bratcher, Robert G., and Nida, Eugene A.
1961 *A Translator's Handbook on Mark*. Leiden: E. J. Brill.

Breech, James
1983 *The Silence of Jesus*. Philadelphia: Fortress.

Brown, Raymond E.
1966 *The Gospel According to John*, Vols. XXIX and XXX. Garden City, New York: Doubleday.

1968 *New Testament Essays*. Garden City, New York. Doubleday.

Browne, Henry
1905 *Handbook of Homeric Study*. New York: Longmans, Green.

Bruce, F. F.
1966 *The Book of Acts*. Grand Rapids: William B. Eerdmans.

Bury, J. B.
1922 "The End of the Odyssey." *Journal of Hellenic Studies* 42: 1–15.

Caird, G. B.
1980 *The Language and Imagery of the Bible*. Philadelphia: Westminster.

Cartlidge, David R., and Dungan, David L.
1980 *Documents for the Study of the Gospels*. Philadelphia: Fortress.

Chariton
  1939   *Chaereas and Callirhoe.* Ann Arbor: University of Michigan.

Clarke, Howard W.
  1967   *The Art of the Odyssey.* Englewood Cliffs, New Jersey: Prentice Hall.

Cranfield, C. E. B.
  1953   *The Gospel According to Saint Mark.* Cambridge: University Press.

Crossan, J. D.
  1973   "Mark and the Relatives of Jesus." *Novum Testamentum* 15 (April): 81–113.
  1978   "A Form for Absence: The Markan Creation of Gospel," in William A. Beardslee, ed., *Semeia* 12. Missoula: Scholars.

Culley, Robert
  1976   *Studies in the Structure of Hebrew Narrative.* Philadelphia: Fortress.

Culpepper, Alan
  1978   "The Passion and Resurrection in Mark." *Review and Expositor* 75 (Fall): 583–600.

Danker, F. W.
  1964   "Meander and the New Testament." *New Testament Studies* 10 (April): 365–368.

Davis, Charles T.
  1980   "A Multidimensional Criticism of the Gospels," in Richard A. Spencer, ed., *Orientation by Disorientation.* Pittsburgh: Pickwick.

Demetrius
  1902   *Demetrius on Style.* Cambridge: University Press.

Dionysius of Halicarnassus
  1910   *On Literary Composition.* London: Macmillan.

Duckworth, G. E.
  1966   *Foreshadowing and Suspense in the Epics of Homer, Apollonius, and Vergil.* New York: Haskell House.

Evans, C. F.
  1970   *Resurrection and the New Testament.* Oxford: Oxford University Press.

Farmer, William R.
  1974   *The Last Twelve Verses of Mark*. Cambridge: University Press.

Farrer, Austin
  1951   *A Study in St. Mark*. London: A. and C. Black.

Feder, Lillian, ed.
  1964   *Crowell's Handbook of Classical Literature*. New York: Thomas Y. Crowell.

Forster, E. M.
  1927   *Aspects of the Novel*. New York: Harcourt Brace and World.

Freedman, David Noel
  1977   "Pottery, Poetry, and Prophecy: An Essay on Biblical Poetry." *Journal of Biblical Literature* 96 (March): 5–26.

Friedman, Alan
  1966   *The Turn of the Novel*. London: Oxford University.

Fuller, Reginald
  1980   *The Formation of the Resurrection Narratives*. Philadelphia: Fortress.

Funk, Robert W.
  1966   *Language, Hermeneutics and the Word of God*. New York: Harper and Row.
  1978   "The Forms of the New Testament Healing Miracle Story," in William A. Beardslee, ed., *Semeia* 12. Missoula: Scholars.

Gould, Ezra
  1901   *A Critical and Exegetical Commentary on the Gospel According to St. Mark*. New York: Charles Scribner's Sons.

Goulder, Michael D.
  1978   "Mark XVI 1–8 and Parallels." *New Testament Studies* 24 (June): 235–240.

Grant, Frederick C.
  1951   *The Interpreter's Bible*, Vol. VIII. New York: Abingdon.

Gunkel, Herman
  1901   *The Legends of Genesis*. New York: Schocken.

Hadas, Moses, ed.

1953   *Three Greek Romances*. Garden City, New York: Double-
        day.

Hägg, Tomas
1971   *Narrative Technique in Ancient Greek Romances*. Stock-
        holm: Svenska Institutet i Athen.

Halliday, M. A. K.
1973   *Explorations in the Functions of Language*. New York:
        Elsevier.

Harrison, R. K.
1969   *Introduction to the Old Testament*. Grand Rapids: William
        B. Eerdmans.

Hassan, Ihab
1967   *The Literature of Silence*. New York: Alfred A. Knopf.

Horace
1961   *Ars Poetica*. Cambridge: Harvard University.

Howard, Wilbert F.
1951   *The Interpreter's Bible*, Vol. VIII. New York: Abingdon.

Hunter, A. M.
1965   *The Gospel According to Saint Mark*. Cambridge: Univer-
        sity Press.

Iser, Wolfgang
1978   *The Act of Reading*. Baltimore: The Johns Hopkins Uni-
        versity.

Johnson, Sherman E.
1951   *The Interpreter's Bible*, Vol. VII. New York: Abingdon.

Kealy, Sean P.
1982   *Mark's Gospel: A History of Its Interpretation*. New York:
        Paulist

Keil, C. F., and Delitzsch, F.
        Commentary on the Old Testament, Vol. I. Grand Rapids:
        William B. Eerdmans.

Kelber, Werner
1979   *Mark's Story of Jesus*. Philadelphia: Fortress.

Kermode, Frank
1967   *The Sense of an Ending*. London: Oxford University.
1979   *The Genesis of Secrecy*. Cambridge: Harvard University.

Kirk, G. S.
1965   *Homer and the Epic*. Cambridge: University Press.

Knox, W. L.
  1942   "The Ending of St. Mark's Gospel." *Harvard Theological Review* 35 (January): 13–23.
Kümmel, Werner G.
  1975   *Introduction to the New Testament.* Nashville: Abingdon.
Lane, William L.
  1974   *The Gospel According to Mark.* Grand Rapids: William B. Eerdmans.
Lattimore, Richard
  1951   *The Iliad of Homer.* Chicago: The University of Chicago.
Leon-Dufour, Xavier
  1979   "Exegetes and Structuralists," in Alfred M. Johnson, Jr., ed., *Structuralism and Biblical Hermeneutics.* Pittsburgh: Pickwick.
Lightfoot, R. H.
  1938   *Locality and Doctrine in the Gospels.* London: Hodder and Stoughton.
  1950   *The Gospel Message of Mark.* Oxford: Clarendon.
Longinus
  1965   *On the Sublime.* Cambridge: Harvard University.
Lyons, John
  1971   *Introduction to Theoretical Linguistics.* London: Cambridge University.
Mailloux, Steven
  1982   *Interpretive Conventions: The Reader in the Study of American Fiction.* Ithaca: Cornell University.
Marin, Louis
  1976   "The Women at the Tomb: A Structuralist Analysis of a Gospel Text," in Alfred M. Johnson, Jr., ed., *The New Testament and Structuralism.* Pittsburgh: Pickwick.
Marshall, I. Howard
  1980   *The Acts of the Apostles.* Grand Rapids: William B. Eerdmans.
Marxsen, Willi
  1969   *Mark the Evangelist: Studies on the Redaction History of the Gospel.* Nashville: Abingdon.
Merleau-Ponty, Maurice
  1967   *Das Auge und der Geist.* Reinbek.

Metzger, Bruce M.
    1971   *A Textual Commentary on the Greek New Testament*. New York: United Bible Societies.

Meyer, H. A. W.
    1884   *Critical and Exegetical Hand-book to the Gospels of Mark and Luke*. New York: Funk and Wagnalls.

Miller, D. A.
    1981   *Narrative and Its Discontents*. Princeton: Princeton University.

Momigliano, Arnaldo
    1977   *Essays in Ancient and Modern Historiography*. New York: Columbia University.

Morganthaler, Robert
    1958   *Statistik der neuestestamentlichen Wortschatzes*. Zurich.

Morris, Leon
    1971   *The Gospel According to John*. Grand Rapids: William B. Eerdmans.

Moule, C. F. D.
    1955   "St. Mark XVI.8 Once More." *New Testament Studies* 2 (September): 58–59.
    1965   *The Gospel According to Mark*. Cambridge: University Press.

Nineham, D. E.
    1963   *Saint Mark*. Philadelphia: Westminster.

Page, Denis
    1955   *The Homeric Odyssey*. Oxford: Clarendon.

Pascal, Blaise
    1952   *Pensées*. Chicago: Encyclopedia Britannica.

Patte, Daniel
    1976   *What is Structural Exegesis?* Philadelphia: Fortress.

Perrin, Norman
    1977   *The Resurrection According to Matthew, Mark, and Luke*. Philadelphia: Fortress.
    1982   *The New Testament: An Introduction*. New York: Harcourt Brace Jovanovich.

Petersen, Norman
    1980   "When is the End not the End? Literary Reflections on

the Ending of Mark's Narrative." *Interpretation* 34 (April): 151–166.

Philostratus
1912 *The Life of Apollonius of Tyana*. London: William Heinemann.

Polanyi, Michael
1967 *The Tacit Dimension*. London: Routledge and Kegan Paul.

Propp, V.
1968 *Morphology of the Folktale*. Austin: University of Texas.

Quintilian
1876 *Institutes of Oratory*. London: George Bell.

Rabkin, Eric S.
1973 *Narrative Suspense*. Ann Arbor: University of Michigan.

Ramsay, William M.
1982 *St. Paul the Traveller and Roman Citizen*. Grand Rapids: Baker.

Rhoads, David
1982 "Narrative Criticism and the Gospel of Mark." *The Journal of the American Academy of Religion* 50 (September): 411–434.

Rhoads, David, and Michie, Donald
1975 *Mark as Story: An Introduction to the Narrative of a Gospel*. Philadelphia: Fortress.

Ricoeur, Paul
1975 "Biblical Hermeneutics," in *Semeia* 4. Missoula: Scholars.

Robbe-Grillet, Alain
1965 *For a New Novel*. New York: Grove.

Robinson, J. M.
1962 "Ascension," in *The Interpreter's Dictionary of The Bible*, Vol. I. New York: Abingdon.

Sayers, Dorothy
1963 *The Song of Roland*. Baltimore: Penguin.

Schillebeeckx, Edward C.
1978 *Jesus: An Experiment in Christology*. New York: Seabury.

Schneidau, Herbert
1969 *Sacred Discontent: The Bible and Western Tradition*. Baton Rouge: Louisiana State University.

Schmeling, Gareth L.
  1974   *Chariton*. New York: Twayne.
  1980   *Xenophon of Ephesus*. Boston: Twayne.

Schweizer, Eduard
  1978   "The Portrayal of the Life of Faith in the Gospel of Mark."
          Interpretation 32 (October): 387–399.

Simon, Ulrich
  1975   *Story and Faith in Biblical Narrative*. London: SPCK.

Simpson, Cuthbert A.
  1952   *The Interpreter's Bible*, Vol. I. New York: Abingdon.

Smart, James D.
  1956   *The Interpreter's Bible*, Vol. VI. New York: Abingdon.

Smith, Marion
  1981   "The Composition of Mark 11–16." *Heythorp Journal* 22:
          363–377.

Speiser, E. A.
  1964   *Genesis*. Garden City, New York: Doubleday.

Steiner, George
  1967   *Language and Silence*. New York: Atheneum.

Stockton, Frank
  1972   *The Lady or the Tiger and Other Stories*. New York:
          Irvington.

Talbert, Charles
  1977   *What is a Gospel?* Philadelphia: Fortress.

Tannehill, Robert C., ed.
  1981   Pronouncement Stories," in *Semeia* 20. Chico: Scholars.

Taylor, Vincent
  1955   *The Gospel According to Mark*. New York: Macmillan.

Theissen, Gerd
  1983   *The Miracle Stories of the Early Christian Tradition*. Phil-
          adelphia: Fortress.

Todorov, Tzvetan
  1971   *The Poetics of Prose*. Ithaca: Cornell University.

Trompf, G. W.
  1972   "The First Resurrection Appearance and the Ending of
          Mark's Gospel." *New Testament Studies* 18 (April): 308–
          330.

Tyson, Joseph B.
  1961   "The Blindness of the Disciples in Mark." *Journal of Biblical Literature* 80 (September): 261–268.

Vergil
  1961   *The Aeneid*. New York: Mentor.

Via, Dan O.
  1975   *Kerygma and Comedy in the New Testament*. Philadelphia: Fortress.

Walsh, P. G.
  1982   "How to end an epic." *The Times Higher Education Supplement* (September 24, 1982).

Weeden, Theodore J.
  1968   "The Heresy that Necessitated Mark's Gospel." ZNTW 59: 145–158.
  1971   *Mark: Traditions in Conflict*. Philadelphia: Fortress.

Wilder, Amos
  1964   *Early Christian Rhetoric*. Cambridge: Harvard.

  1980   "The Gospels as Narrative." *Interpretation* 34 (July): 296–299.

Xenophon
  1914   *Cyropaedia*. London: William Heinemann.

Zahn, Theodor
  1909   *Introduction to the New Testament*. Edinburgh: T. and T. Clark.